THE ULTIMATE ROCKET LEAGUE 2V2 GUIDE

Achieve Success With The Pacifist System®

Written and Published
By AirCharged Gaming

Published by Pacifist Press™

ISBN: 978-1-9191799-0-2
Printed on demand worldwide by printing partners on behalf of Pacifist Press™.

First Edition

INDEX

INTRODUCTION

Welcome to **The Ultimate Rocket League 2v2 Guide**! Whether you are just starting out or looking to level up your game, this book is here to help. We will cover the basics, like understanding the roles of **1st man and 2nd man**, how to work together effectively, as well as giving you some useful tips for both defence and offence.

This includes:

- The best drills to develop.
- How to schedule the drills.
- And how to use **The Pacifist System** to have success in 2v2 with a teammate or solo.

The goal in this book is to keep things simple, so you can easily apply what you learn and improve. So many times, you get a resource, and it does not explain exactly what to do in a **step-by-step** format, so you feel like you do not have a solid game plan. This book will be an exception and will provide more practical help than any other resource in Rocket League, that is a promise!

In the chapters ahead, you will find some solid advice and strategies that top players actually use. Allowing you to read the game better and start making smarter plays. The goal is to help you climb the ranks, one step at a time with a complete system.

"Players that struggle, focus on their goal (outcome). Players that succeed focus on a system (process)."

In the next page you will learn more about me and my background to give you confidence of the methods in this book, as they may go completely against common information spread on Reddit, Discord and in popular YouTube videos.

When **The Pacifist System** was first created it was heavily criticised. Today, it is recognised as the strongest system in Rocket League, with many of the developments starting to appear in professional play. This system allows players to stay one step ahead of the competition.

WHO AM I?

I am Dave, also known as **AirCharged**, a **Rocket League coach**, **player**, and **commentator** who originally purchased Rocket League just two weeks after release. I have achieved **Grand Champion (GC) rewards for over 20 seasons** and have completed several no mechanics to GC series in 1s, 2s and 3s.

I have peaked at **GC3 Division 3** a handful of times and have been fortunate enough to work with many top 100 players through:

- 5 years of coaching, commentary and sponsored tournaments.
- 8 years of Rocket League content creation.
- And over 10 years of Rocket League play.

Before being a Rocket League player, I was a top ranked **Team Fortress Classic (TFC)** player, a Half-Life mod and capture-the-flag game. This was one of the early eSports, an 8v8 format where half the team attacked to secure the opponent's flag, while the other half defended. As you can imagine, I played defence.

In TFC, I became nicknamed by the community as the **'King of Air Shots'**, which inspired me to put 'Air' before my original online name 'Charged'.

After TFC I became a **semi-professional basketball player** in the UK and a **competitive jiu-jitsu grappler**. In both of these sports I managed to perform well purely from my ability to read the actions of others, and this is one thing I hope to share with you in this book.

The strategies I learnt growing up and competing in a multitude of sports are the same strategies I use in Rocket League.

And overtime I have refined them further through:

- Studying replays.
- Using statistics.
- And doing **over 1,000 hours of coaching** (estimated 1,148 hours so far).

By day, I work as an **analyst in a marketing department**, this reflects my obsession with numbers, data, and evidence-based decision-making.

Everything you will read from here will be the lessons I have learned over the past 10 years, designed to help you on your journey.

Let's do this!

THE FOUR MAIN SITUATIONS

Rocket League is a complex game, especially when the game is not broken down into common situations and understandable circumstances.

To help with this, I look at Rocket League in four main situations. Understanding these situations allows the player to recognise what overarching strategy to use. From there, they can apply core fundamentals to win in that area.

The four main situations in Rocket League are:

1. Offensive Defence – Defending the opponent in their half, when they have possession of the ball. This is where you ideally want to **full-map shadow** and block the centre, **funnelling the opponent toward the corner** to limit their attack.
2. Offensive Offence – When you have the ball in the opponent's half and are actively attacking. Forcing difficult saves, stealing boost, and applying pressure to keep them pinned into defensive positions.
3. Defensive Defence – When the ball is in your half, and you are being shot at. Forced to defend difficult plays and react carefully.
4. Defensive Offence – When you are trying to break out of your own half. You have the possession and are trying to begin building an attack.

One of the most important things to remember is, **do not try to attack if your team does not have possession**.

By this, I mean, if the opponents have possession, your goal should be to **force them to play the ball into a position that is hard to score from**. Such as the corner.

This makes it far easier to defend and counter.

What often happens is that players dive on opponents who clearly have possession, and they end up **missing, getting beaten, or countered**.

Offensive Defence

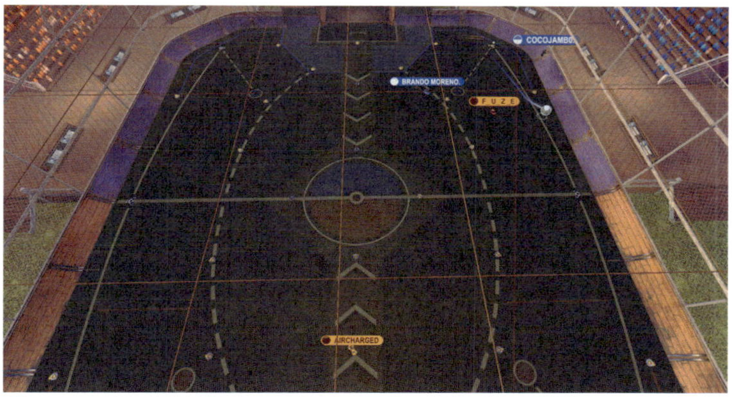

Offensive Offence

Defensive Defence

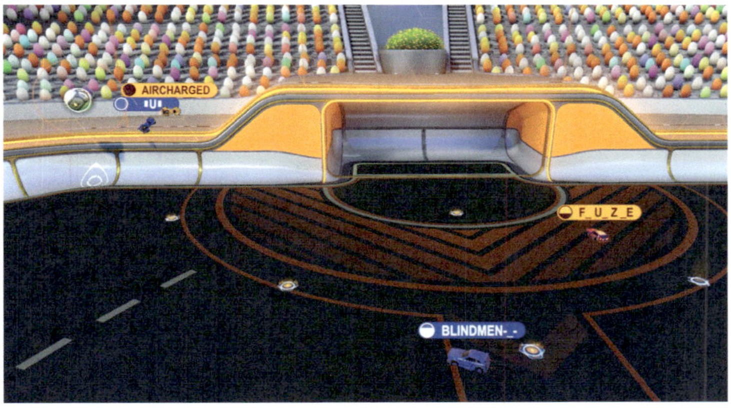

Defensive Offence

THE FUNDAMENTAL RULES

Now we understand the different situations, let's go over a list of the core fundamentals. Next to each fundamental will be either OD, OO, DD, DO, which refers to the initials of the 4 main situations, so you know where these fundamentals is most likely to apply.

These fundamental rules are important to follow as closely as possible.

The closer they are followed the more successful you will be. Some of these fundamentals are more 'valuable' than others, and when broken, create what I call '**Majors**'.

Less 'valuable' fundamentals will create what I call '**Minors**' when they are broken.

This means some mistakes have a bigger impact on the game than others. They will be **highlighted in purple**.

Minor vs Major

In UK driving tests, we have **Major and Minor incidents**.

When taking your driving test, you are allowed up to 15 **Minor** faults and can still pass. However, just one **Major** fault and it is an instant failure.

I take a similar approach in Rocket League.

You can make **multiple small errors**, like not following up on kick-off, and potentially be fine.

However, one Major mistake, like flipping full-speed into the opponent's corner as 2nd man with 0 boost, and it **should be a goal for the opponents**.

Never a good idea - Look how open the map is for our counterattack (which we scored).

The Fundamentals For 2v2

1. **Do not carry out of defence without any vision.** (DO)
    a. If you have accidentally caught the ball in front of your net and cannot see, either flick or drop the ball and jump for a low 50 immediately.
    b. If you are near the ball on the ground and cannot see any opponents, single jump immediately.
    c. If the ball has gone above your head in a dangerous area, jump up and touch it, ideally high and into the corner to waste time whilst you recover.
    d. If you are in your corner, be cautious about pushing the ball up the wall if the opponents are already on it, as you will likely get dunked.
2. **Use vision to decide what to do as 2nd man**, if the ball hits the backboard you must go, unless you can clearly see opponent's 2nd man is not available by using car cam. (DD, DO)
3. **Do not dive into corners**, especially the opponents. (OD, OO)
4. **Do not be aggressive with 0 boost.** (OD, DO, OO)
5. **Avoid facing the play as a 1st man** when defending for prolonged periods (over 2 seconds) as you lose mobility. (OD)
6. **Do not end up in the opponent's net.** (OO)
7. **Always get a 'hand in the face'** (hover when the opponent is air dribbling) to pressure them. (OD, DD)
8. **1st man grabs big pads and also covers backboard.** (DD, DO)
9. **2nd man waits for their turn.** Try and wait for your turn instead of actively looking for a way in. (DD, DO)
10. **Match the height of the ball on the wall** to gain vision and prevent dunks / demos. (DD, DO, OO)
11. **Pressure / pick up an uncontested ball** - front end aggression (THIS DOES NOT MEAN DIVE IN! INSTEAD DRIVE CLOSE FIRST!). (OD, DO, OO)
12. **Do not fake out of goal-side.** (OD, DD, DO, OO)
13. **Make your fakes look real**, like a true challenge. (OD, DD, DO, OO)
14. **Be flexible.** Just because you intend to fake, does not mean you have to, be willing to potentially challenge, drive challenge, or steal possession as you get closer and gain more information. (OD, DD, DO, OO)
15. **For 50/50s, where possible, take them from inside to outside.** (OD, DD, DO)
16. **Do not dive at walls, or shoot the ball recklessly into them**, as the ball will bounce centre whilst you stick to the wall. (OD, DD)
17. **Do not dive in as last man.** (OD, DD, OO)
18. **Do not force the offence.** (DO)

Now we have covered the individual and team fundamentals, we can use them to guide our understanding of our roles in 2v2. Specifically as **1st man and 2nd man**.

THE FUNDAMENTAL ROLES

Before we talk about **drills and skills in 2s**, it is important to have an overview of the **key fundamental roles** for each position in Rocket League.

In my opinion, the way most of the player base currently plays is **outdated.**

They use a rotation-based system that leads to **less enjoyment**, **more frustration**, and **no real understanding** of what's happening on the field.

So, below are the **core skills and responsibilities** required for both **1st and 2nd man**, the two primary roles in **2v2 play**.

1st Man Roles

The 1st man is your offensive powerhouse, controlling the flow of the game. Here is how you can make the most of this role:

- **Create a 2v1** – Use positioning and pressure to force your opponents into a disadvantageous situation, giving you control of the ball.
- **Control the Game** – Stay involved with the play and dictate the pace. Use your presence to pressure opponents and control space.
- **Stay Close and Use Presence** – Always stay close to the ball when attacking or defending. This prevents the opposing team from easily clearing the ball.
- **Protect the Middle** – As the 1st man, keep an eye on the middle of the field and prevent easy passes that could lead to scoring chances.
- **Funnel the Ball to the Corner on Defence** – If you are on defence, guide the ball toward the corner, reducing the opponent's offensive options.
- **Support the 2nd Man** – Always be ready to cover for the 2nd man and assist when needed.
- **Mobility is Key** – Stay side-on to the ball as much as possible. This keeps you agile and prevents you from getting outplayed. Avoid facing the ball head-on, unless using front-end aggression, as it limits your movement and vision.
- **Do Not Dodge Unless Necessary** – Try and stay grounded as much as possible so you can avoid unnecessary 50/50s and move into where the ball is being hit.

2nd Man Roles

The 2nd man is responsible for supporting the 1st man and covering critical areas of the field:

- **Protect the 1st Man** – When the 1st man is pushing, ensure the net and centre is protected.
- **Move Forward into Loose Balls** – Always be ready to step into the play if a loose ball comes your way, but do not force it.
- **Green Zone** – As the 2nd man, you will often move centrally. Focus on getting into positions where you can capitalise on free opportunities to score.
- **Read the Play** – When the opponents are collapsed, you can be pushed forward in a central position. When the opponents are attacking or about to have a hard 50 with your teammate, you need to be further back, also central.
- **Try Not to Overuse Flips** – You want to stay ready to react, so save your flips for moments where they will give you a real advantage.
- **Watch the Opponent's 2nd Man** – Keep an eye on their 2nd man, this can give you insights into their plays and tactics.

As 2nd man in defence, I am waiting for my opportunity, but not getting involved and messing up my 1st man.

THE PACIFIST STRATEGY

Now that we understand the fundamental rules, the severity of breaking them, and the goals of each role, we can begin using a **systematic approach** to stay aligned with the fundamentals while executing our roles.

These **fundamentals and roles** come from hours upon hours of **playing, casting, coaching, and analysing** Rocket League. This has allowed me to identify **clear trends** in where teams succeed, and where they fail. These methods have been **extensively tested across all ranks** and are even **utilised in RLCS play**.

The Pacifist System was built on the foundation of these rules. At one point, I had a notebook full of Rocket League strategies, and the **only survivor** was **The Pacifist System**. Since then, it has been **refined and evolved into the structured system** you are about to learn.

The reason it was called **The Pacifist System** was that there was a **heavy emphasis on not challenging, or attacking the ball when we did not own it**, this is something that is totally different to traditional play.

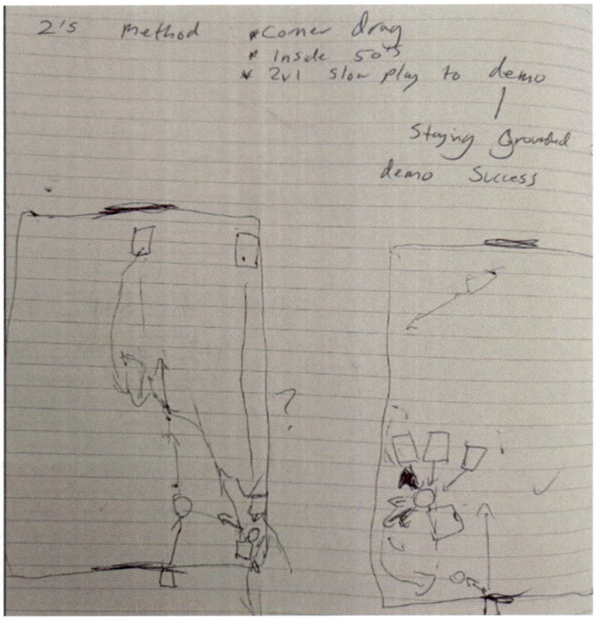

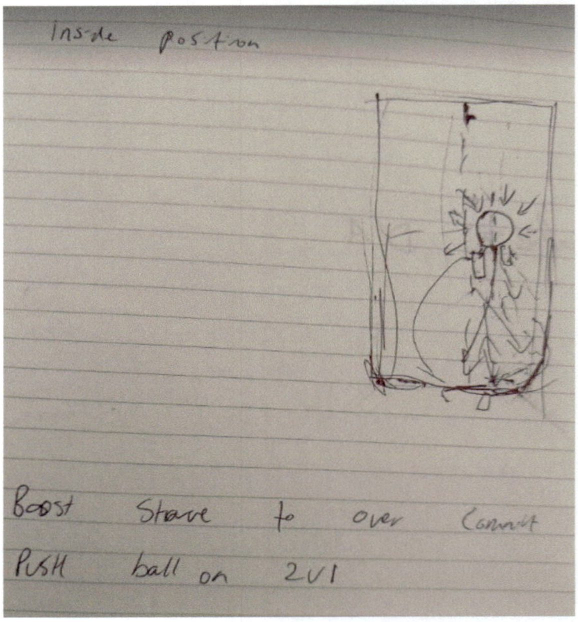

Original notes from 2017.

Overarching Strategy

The overarching strategy behind **The Pacifist System** is to consistently create **2v1 situations**. The more 2v1s we generate, the more opportunities we have to **apply pressure, maintain possession**, and build **prolonged attacks**.

By sustaining pressure, we can begin to **boost starve** the opponent and gain **map control**, leading to more effective and repeatable offensive opportunities.

To create 2v1s, we must focus on either:

- **Separating the defenders**, or
- **Forcing both into high-risk situations** that could lead to **Major errors**.

As we improve, we will also learn to punish Minor errors and build plays from smaller advantages.

To do that, when starting out we **create a simple funnel**. This way we take them away from the **centre (green zone)** and into the **wings** (**red zone**).

A Rocket League pitch has **three zones, green, orange and red**. Green is where we want to spend the **majority of our time** as it allows reactivity towards any loose ball. Defensively it is also the **most dangerous place** to allow the opponent to move into. To prevent the opponents accessing the green zone, we funnel them from an inside position to our corner, keeping them pinned into the red zone.

The Various zones on a Rocket League pitch.

DEFENCE - 1ST MAN

In the system, the **1st man** is the player who stays **extremely close to the bal**l and focuses on **establishing control**. Rather than diving forward aggressively, their goal is to **defend with momentum moving toward their own net** as much as possible.

The reason for this is simple, it allows them to **reload their challenge**. For example, if they lose a 50/50, with their positioning and momentum toward their net makes it easier to **recover and challenge again**.

This is much more effective than diving in and relying on a single, all-or-nothing touch.

The Funnel Defensive Strategy

Many players shadow on the **outside** of the ball and funnel opponents towards their own net, hoping to make a save at the last second.

The issue with this approach is that **one slight mistake = a goal**, or worse, you bump into your teammate and cause chaos.

In **The Pacifist System**, we defend by **funnelling the opponent toward either of our corners**, however usually we aim for the corner on the same side that the play started on. This constantly limits their offensive options and builds frustration.

Consider this, every time your opponent has attacked in the past, they have likely faced defenders who dive or shadow in the usual way. This has led to **thousands of hours** attacking the same type of defence.

Now, by changing the setup completely, and **funnelling them into the corner**, we force them into a situation they have **barely ever practiced**.

That gives **you** the advantage.

While your opponent has minimal exposure to this style, you will have already accumulated hours of experience defending this way. You will learn the patterns, anticipate the outcomes, and build confidence.

It is like being a **southpaw boxer**:

- A southpaw has trained against hundreds of orthodox fighters.
- But the orthodox fighter has barely seen a southpaw.
- The result? A built-in advantage.

Once the funnel is successful and the ball is in the corner:

- 1st man stays near the ball, on the inside.
- 2nd man sits deep in net, watching for the dive.

From here, only two things can happen:

1. The opponent **backs off,** giving us space to set up a quality offence.
2. The opponent **dives**, and our **2nd man** is ready to counter hard toward their net.

To funnel effectively, make sure you are **positioned on the inside** of the opponent's approach and not the outside.

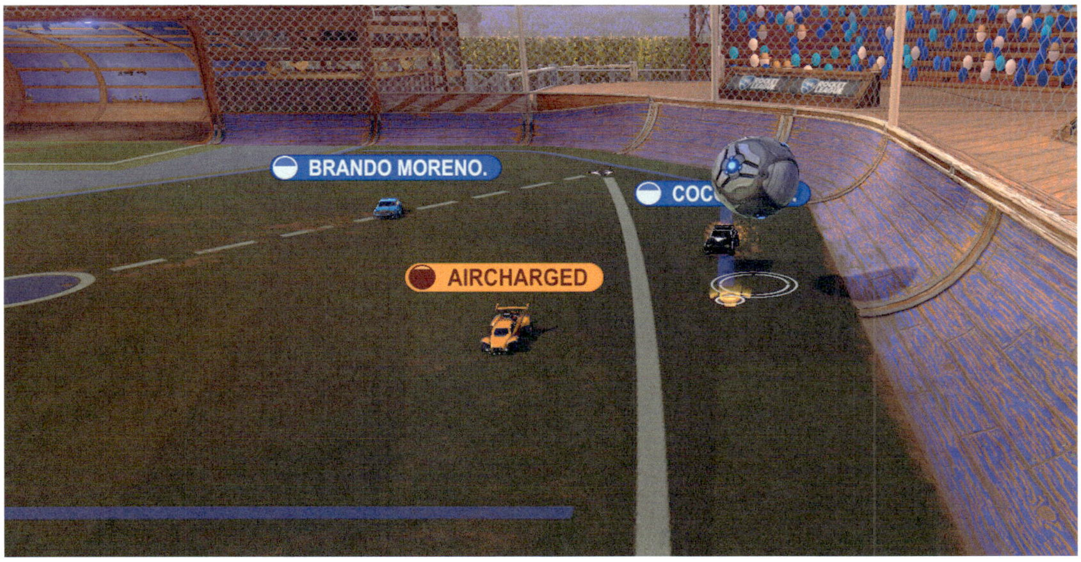

Inside position forces the opponent to play the ball to our corner.

Outside position forces the opponent to the middle, more dangerous unless using triangle defending.

Front-end Aggression

Before we move onto the various methods of shadowing and positioning, it is important to introduce a key principle known as **front-end aggression**.

When players first learn this system, they are often far too passive, giving up too much space. Ironically, that is exactly why this system was created: to prevent giving space away for free.

So, to help fix that, as the **1st man**, you need to be aggressive when it is your time to engage. As soon as your teammate rotates out, or it becomes your turn to step into the 1st man role, try to **get as close as possible** to the opponent with the ball, without hitting the ball (unless you see a gap)!

The idea is to either find a gap to take the ball as you arrive, or **turn into an instant inside shadow**.

This pressure is what we call **front-end aggression**, and it is something you will use constantly, both when you are the 1st man and when you are rotating into it.

The key to successful front-end aggression is making sure you power slide in the correct direction. Done right, you will cut down space quickly and create extra pressure.

Which way you turn depends on the opponent's position relative to the ball:

- **If they're on the outside of the ball**, turn towards the middle.
- **If they're on the inside of the ball**, turn towards the outside.

This blocks their immediate path and triggers a 'fight or flight' reaction, they will either hit the ball into you or freeze. Rarely will you face someone composed enough to take it in the opposite direction, and if they do, it is fine, you can easily adjust.

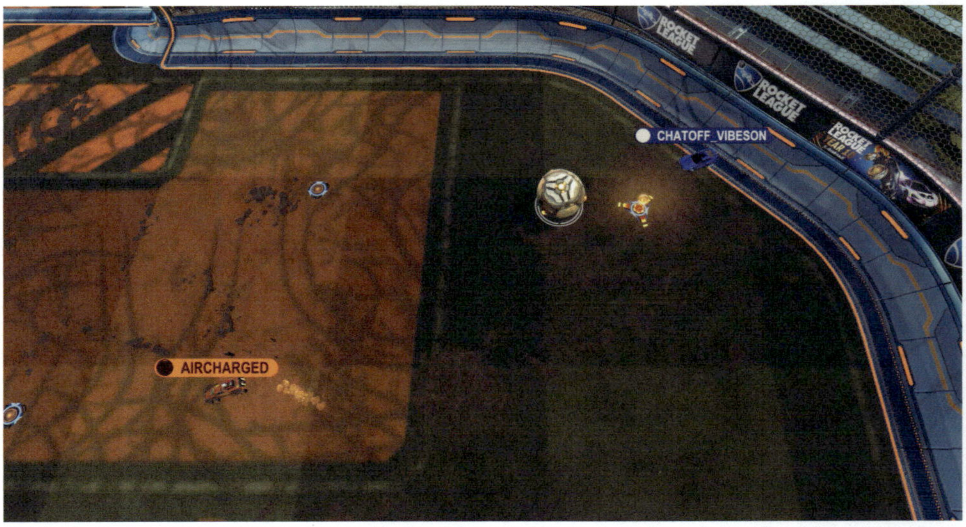

Notice I have turned to the inside as the opponent is on the outside of the ball.

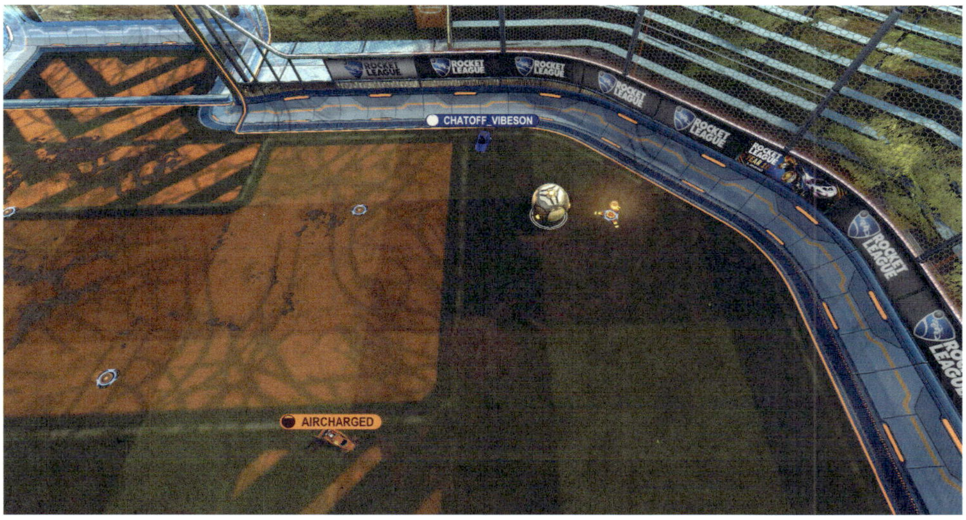

Notice I have turned to the outside as the opponent is on the inside of the ball.

Inside Vs. Inline Vs. Outside Position

In Rocket League, there are three main methods of shadowing, **inside, inline** and **outside**.

Outside Position

As previously discussed, the **outside shadow** is the more typical method. It involves positioning yourself **between the ball and the wall** (see image below) and **curving in** toward the net to close the attacker off and challenge or take the ball.

Opponent outside and allowing the middle to be taken.

This method is solid, and, when mixed into your playstyle, can be extremely valuable, especially in **1v1**. However, in **2v2**, funnelling the ball toward your own net can lead to **confusion for your teammate**, and gives the **opponent's 1st man** an easier read and opportunity to challenge or demo.

Inline Position

Nearly all shadowing ends in an **inline position** (also known as **goal-side shadowing**), where you are **directly in line** with the ball's path.

This style can be **very powerful**:

- It allows you to **hide challenges** behind the ball.
- You can **block ground shots without moving**, as the ball will simply hit you.

An inline shadow is when you are directly in front of the ball, following it's path.

However, inline shadowing is not without risk:

- It offers **fewer counterattack opportunities**, especially in **1v1**.
- You are more vulnerable to being **air dribble bumped** or **50/50'd**, as you are often static and lack momentum to respond quickly.
- It can also end in you driving directly at your teammate if you have given the opponent the centre of the field.

Inside Position

The **inside position** is not as widely used as outside shadowing, though it is becoming more popular, especially among top players like **Zen, M0nkey M00n, BeastMode, and Rw9**.

This method involves staying **between the ball and the centre of the pitch**, allowing you to **pressure the opponent toward the corner**. If the opponent tries to shoot through the narrow inside gap, they are often handing your teammate a **free ball**.

There are more advanced techniques where players switch back and forth between inside and outside positions, a method known as '**snaking**'. However, for now, your focus should be on **mastering the fundamentals** of inside positioning.

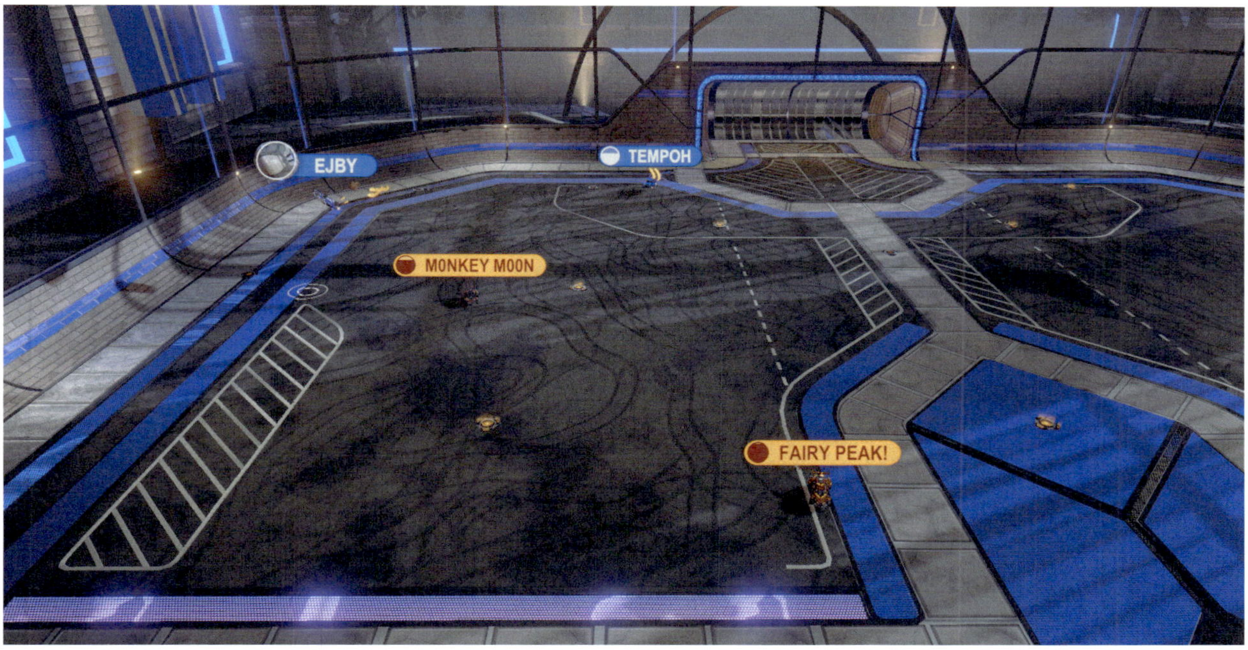

The Pacifist System is now being regularly spotted in professional play. Although, when I first created it, many said it would not work in the higher ranks.

The inside position is powerful because it **forces a decision** out of your opponent:

- They either push themselves and the ball into the **corner**, which is what we want, a successful funnel.
- Or they try to go **through or over you**, which can lead to 50s or wasted possessions.

How To Challenge A Ball

Challenging a ball in Rocket League should always be done in a **high-percentage fashion**, especially within **The Pacifist System**.

When you challenge, you generally have two main approaches:

- **Face the opponent's side** of the pitch and dive at the ball (typical aggressive challenge).
- Or **face your own side**, challenging **on your way back toward your half** (often safer and more recoverable).

This challenge is risky, even if the blue team win the challenge, the ball will go directly to the orange teams 2nd man.

M0nkey M00n using shadow defending to defend towards his own net, this led to a successful defensive stop, and possession for the orange team.

Face-out Challenge

A **face-out challenge** is one of the riskiest plays in Rocket League. If you miss, you are not just out of position, you are completely out of the play. What makes it worse is that the chance of missing is **extremely high**, especially if the opponent has already **established control** or has some level of **vision**.

Take, for example, **Gamers8**, where in the final we saw **BeastMode and Daniel vs. Rw9 and Killeerrz**. BeastMode and Daniel **shadowed** and **funnelled the ball to the corner** before building up their offence. In contrast, Rw9 and Killeerrz **dived a total of 14 times**, and only **1** of those was a successful challenge.

Even at the **top level**, diving is rarely a good strategy. While there are occasional exceptions that lead to success, I can tell you from watching **thousands of hours** of players at **all ranks (including pros)** that face-out challenges generally **do not work out**.

That said, there are **specific scenarios** where face-out challenges are **more viable**:

- **If you are 1st man** against the **opponent's 2nd man**, a challenge can be worth the risk.
    - **If you win**, you are likely scoring.
    - **If you lose**, you often have time to recover.
- **If the ball is grounded** and you are the **1st man**, diving in is **less dangerous** since the number of outplays available to your opponent is limited.
- **Challenging early**, before your opponent gets their **control touch**, can work, but be cautious. Some players **fake control** or **immediately flick**, leaving you **overcommitted** (imagine a **tail-whip flick**).
- **If you are stuck in net** and facing a shot on target, diving to block can be your **best option**, especially if it is a **fast power shot** that you cannot shadow or save conventionally.
- If you are **highly experienced at reading the game**, you can sometimes challenge once the opponent has **locked into a path** and committed to their line.
- And of course, **turning your car sideways** when 50/50ing can reduce the risk of losing heavily.

But here is the question you need to ask:

What do you gain from this?

In most cases:

- You are giving yourself a **huge chance to miss**.
- Even if you hit the ball, you will likely **send it away from yourself**, meaning you have given up possession.

It is easy to tap the ball around a diving player.

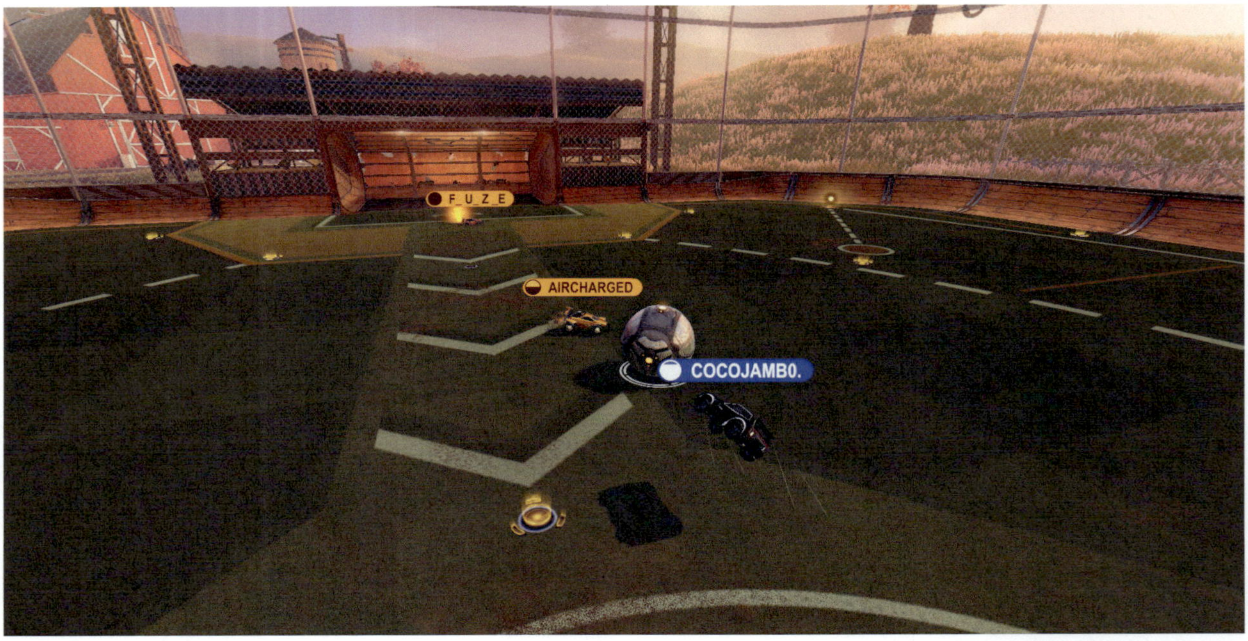

Even if COCO gets a solid hit on the ball, they are going to either hit it at us, or it will go to our corner, either way, we will end up with the possession.

Face-away (Shadow) Challenge

A **face-away challenge** is when you are **facing your own net or away from the ball** as you challenge. This might feel counterintuitive, but the **percentage of success is much higher** than face-out dives.

Now, you might argue that you are helping the opponents by pushing the ball toward your own side. However, it is important to understand this key point:

You are bringing the ball closer to safety.

By guiding the ball toward the corner and **moving with it**, you are often taking it away from the opponent. Once the ball reaches the corner, **the scoring angle is gone**, meaning you have neutralised the threat.

If the ball **accidentally goes central** (which we try to avoid), the opponent should still not have **clear possession** to finish the attack. In these cases, **our 2nd man** should be in a position to step in and **take over the play**.

There are also things you can do to increase success with face-away (or shadow) challenges, for example, using the **Perfect Side Flip** to block more angles and reduce the chance of getting dunked or outplayed.

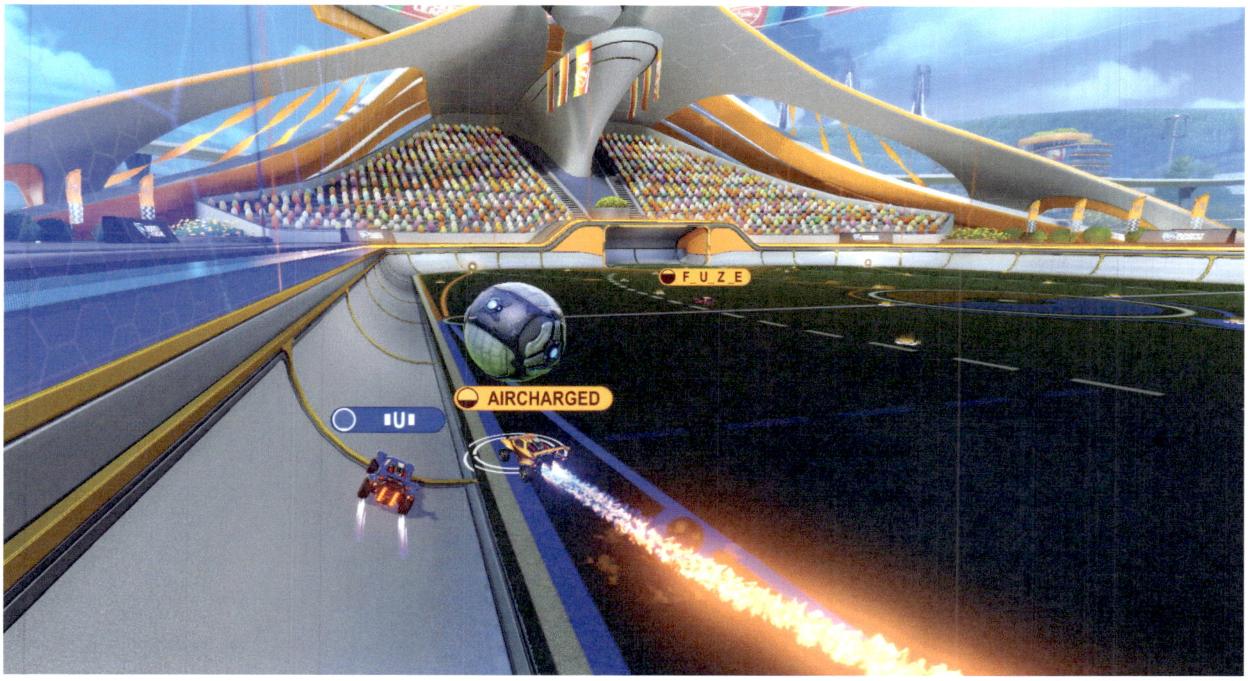

By challenging the ball on the way back, I can take it back to my teams corner, and grab all the boosts, forcing the blue opponent to be in my half with 0 boost, ready for a counterattack.

Preventing Attacks, Forcing The Funnel

To excel in this strategy, it is important to **deny the opponent access to bouncing balls, carries, or anything that could go over you.** While The Pacifist System is designed to handle these threats, often allowing the **2nd man to clean up** if the ball is on target, our aim is to **protect the 2nd man as much as possible** and **frustrate the opponent's rhythm**.

To help with this, we can often shut down attacks early by using a simple but powerful technique: **The Perfect Side Flip**.

The Perfect Side Flip

The **Perfect Side Flip** is the **strongest defensive flip in the game**, and for good reason. Let's first consider the other flips:

- **Front flip** – This causes you to flip **away from the opponent** when shadowing, giving them more map space.
- **Diagonal flip** – You **cannot boost through a diagonal flip**, so you are more likely to get demoed.
- **Back flip** – This is a **committed play**, and if you miss, you have left your teammate completely alone.

With a **side flip**, you can **boost while flipping**, and you move **across the ball from an inside to outside position**. This allows you to simultaneously make the ball awkward and **avoid demo or bump attempts**.

Now, while this sounds simple, it is probably the **hardest move you will learn defensively**, because it must be perfect. This means that wherever your nose is facing when you begin your side flip, it must continue to face in that exact direction when you finish the side flip. The way to do this, is to only input the direction in the joystick at the **exact moment you input the dodge**.

You need to be **completely straight or even turned slightly away** so your side flip pushes the ball safely outward, this is known as an open defensive position. An **imperfect side flip** often fails because it directs the ball poorly or gets you demoed due to turning in towards the direction you want to flip.

To avoid hitting the ball into the wall (which causes it to bounce off dangerously while you are stuck in a dodge animation, or against the wall), aim to hit **just above the midpoint of the ball.** This way, the ball will be pushed **downward and roll up the wall** toward safety. However, try not to do this too close to the wall, as you will end up landing awkwardly. To avoid such a situation, if the ball has bounce and you are close to the wall, you can use a single/ double jump to guide the ball toward the corner whilst killing the bounces.

You might worry this setup allows the opponent to aerial, but if done correctly, the ball moves so quickly **into your corner** that **it only appears this way**. In reality, it is **just out of reach**.

With the Perfect Side Flip you finish the flip facing the same direction you started.

Many viewers of my series ask, *"How come your opponents never aerial like mine?"*.

The truth is, **I feed them balls just out of reach**, using fundamentals they have never trained against.

Take the **Perfect Side Flip**, which is **always done from inside position to outside position**. The opponent pushes the ball, and I side flip perfectly. The ball climbs the wall while maintaining or even **gaining forward momentum**. This triggers a **false aerial attempt**, where the opponent thinks they can reach it, but they cannot.

Even though the ball cannot be aerial'd safely, the opponent will feel they can and still try. This forces an over commit and an easy counterattack.

Now let's look at what most players do, the **Imperfect Side Flip**.

They **turn into the ball before flipping**, which changes the direction of the flip and **pushes the ball back and up**, stabilizing it. This creates a **perfect aerial setup** for your opponent.

With the Imperfect Side Flip, I start by facing the net, and finish facing the wall.

Worse still, the **Imperfect Side Flip** leaves you vulnerable to **demos or bumps**, giving the opponent even more time and confidence.

The **earlier** you can execute a Perfect Side Flip, the better. Doing it as the opponent collects the ball can **shut down flicks and bounce dribbles** before they start.

You want to **jump fairly high**, just above the midpoint of the ball, so it rolls **smoothly up the wall and toward the corner**.

Using the perfect side flip also pushes you sideways, if timed right you can use it to dodge through boosts and further starve the opponent.

If you jump too low, the ball will **centre**, and you will end up **on the outside**, a very weak position.

This side flip is bad, its imperfect and I hit the ball too low, this means it will bounce into the middle and I will stick to the ball.

The aftermath, I got lucky that they went ahead of the ball, but in 2v2, this would be a goal. So ensure not to hit the ball that low. If you really cannot perform the side flip safely, due to a high bounce, use a single jump just to prevent it coming into the middle.

Pincer Movement

The **pincer movement** is essentially a step-by-step method to close down an offensive player. You want to **turn and drive at the player**, then **straighten up**, then **pincer in**, then straighten up again, repeating this pattern until you are close enough to land a **perfect side flip**.

With practice, you will be able to do this quickly, often needing just **one clean pincer movement**.

The reason we use this method is simple:

If you drive **directly** at the ball from a side position, it is too easy for the opponent to **demo you** or force you into an **imperfect side flip**, which causes your car to move across the opponent, rather than matching their momentum. That mismatch is what gets you deleted, or dunked.

Using the pincer movement to close the distance, I would not dive across like this though, I need to straighten up first.

I have now straightened up, one more and I will be close enough to use a perfect side flip.

Being Safe In The Corner And Matching The Height Of The Ball

Once the ball is in your corner, or retreating toward it, the priority is staying safe. There are a few subtle but powerful habits that can help you do this effectively.

The first is positioning. Do not just take the **inside line in front of the ball** when it is going up the corner, also make sure you are **slightly above** it. This does two things:

1. It puts the **ball between you and your opponent**, acting as a shield. If they try to demo you, they will hit the ball first, which usually slows them down enough to take away their **supersonic speed**.
2. It makes it almost impossible for them to get the ball over you, forcing them into awkward plays. You are now funnelling the ball down toward your teammate, either they **back off, force a bad 50/50**, or **play it low** where your teammate is ready to intercept.

Being above the ball in this manner allows you to protect the high backboard, and get vision easily.

Remember: Always match the height of the ball on the **defensive wall** or **backboard** or stay slightly above it.

However, avoid doing this when the ball is in **open space** on the wall, like mid-map or in the opponent's corner. In those areas, staying on the wall **leaves the middle exposed**. Instead, use quick flashes up the wall before the opponent is able to touch the ball, to make your presence known, then drop back down. This visual pressure creates doubt in the opponent's mind, even if you do not challenge.

This defensive positioning is commonly used as people tend to focus on defending the corner and leaving the net open. This costs even high ranked players unnecessary goals.

The Backboard

Matching the height of the ball or being above the ball on the backboard is imperative.

As you improve, opponents will become sneakier, mixing up their challenges to throw you off. To counter this, when you are **on the backboard**, hold a strong **inside position** and **match the height of the ball, or even be slightly higher than the ball**, this allows you to start to mix up your responses too.

You can **single jump** to block a ball rolling around the corner to keep it stuck to the wall. Or you can use a **backflip** or even a **half-flip** to knock the ball gently back toward the corner and turn defence into attack.

This is especially effective when the opponent is **lurking directly beneath you**, or if they have committed to **demoing your second man**, giving you the opportunity to reset the play or catch them off guard.

Triangle Defending

There is another defensive method we can use, but it should only be used when we have a **boost advantage**.

As mentioned previously, funnelling from the inside to the outside is a sure-fire way to improve defensive success, but sometimes, you will want to get onto **offence right away**, and that is when triangle defending comes in. This is most effective when you have managed to **boost starve the opponent**.

If you are able to grab the opponent's corner boost and you know they are low on boost, you can **triangle defend**.

This method, instead of funnelling from inside to outside, does the opposite, it funnels the opponent **from outside to inside**. This forces them to take the middle, where the boost is harder to grab, they are more exposed, and where a 50/50 challenge leaves you in a stronger position. The 50/50 should be in your advantage as the opponent will push the ball forward, meaning when you side flip you barrel the ball over them. However, if it spills to either side, you can easily react.

The reason we call this **triangle defending** is that the movement of the play forms the shape of a triangle.

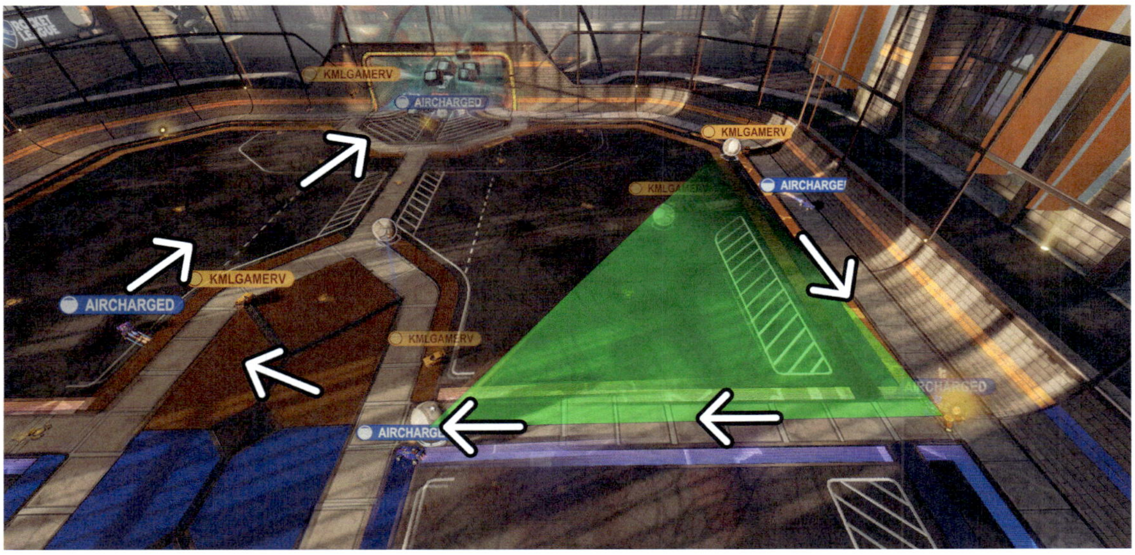

Triangle defending can lead to easy goals when performed correctly.

To perform this defence, after successfully starving the opponent, **head toward the middle boost**. This makes the opponent feel less pressure and often causes them to push into the middle blindly. As they move in, begin **collapsing into the centre**, where you can meet their path with a side flip.

Then, instantly react to where the ball spills out and get onto the offence.

Snaking

An effective way to take the ball off a player is to use a technique known as '**Snaking**'. This was originally used by **Paschy90** in the early days of the game, but was later refined and popularised by **oKhalid**. Snaking is essentially multiple **fakes on the ball**, but each time from a different **shadow position**, alternating between inside and outside.

To snake, a player will begin in a **shadow position** and then turn in toward the ball, hiding themselves behind it. To the dribbler, this often looks like a challenge is about to happen, which forces them to make a play early. However, if they do not bite on the fake, the defender will pop out on the **other side** and repeat the movement.

What makes this so powerful is that, at **any moment**, the defender can **actually challenge** if the opponent fails to react to the fakes.

Snaking is an **advanced move**, but it can be practiced and improved in a relatively short time. To begin snaking, you might first want to practice on a **still ball**, moving back and forth between **inside and outside shadows**, essentially making a **figure-8** movement.

Using snaking to get the opponent to bite and throw the ball away from themselves.

Tap power slide as you turn in toward the ball and use **a small burst of boost** so it looks like you are about to dive. Use only a little boost, when players are first learning how to do this, they often drain all their boost within seconds.

Snaking is a good option when you are **unable to get close** to an opponent, specifically on the side, as they have already established control. If you cannot pincer in for a side flip, and you are not in position to defend from behind, therefore are in front of the opponent, **snaking gives you a way to apply pressure** and force a mistake, **without overcommitting**.

Stealing The Ball

As you get better at all the previous techniques, you will find it easier to steal the ball from opponents and maintain possession for your team. Over time, opponents will become so frustrated that they will start smashing the ball away just to stop you from locking them down, which is exactly what we want. This often results in your 2nd man getting easy possession, giving your team another strong opportunity to attack.

Defending From Behind

One of the most effective and underused ways to **regain possession** is by defending from behind the opponent. This typically happens after a **deep fake, drive challenge**, or **demo attempt**, situations where you have ended up **behind the play** instead of insta-shadowing.

Rather than immediately leaving the play, we deliberately **stay on the ball**. From this position behind the opponent, you have two strong options:

1. Go for a **demo from behind** to neutralise the threat.
2. Or **knock the ball back** toward your own corner or side wall to safely reset possession

Both options disrupt the opponent's control and allow you to **take back the ball** while they are still recovering.

This technique turns what looks like a lost play into a **counterattack or rese**t, giving you control without needing a standard rotation.

Using defending from behind to get the demo and a free ball. This is the most common form of defending at the higher ranks.

The Drag Back

As mentioned earlier, a **drag back** can be a highly effective option when **transitioning between offence and defence**. It involves **deliberately taking the ball back into your own half** when you are unable to generate meaningful offence. Unlike standard retreating defence, this time **you initiate the retreat**, bringing the ball with you to **reset the play**.

Another ideal moment to use a drag back is when **the ball bounces behind you**. Many players instinctively **turn around the ball to re-face the opponent's net**. However, in doing so, they often **lose sight of the opponent** and get **dunked** as they rotate into the ball. In these moments, **dragging the ball back is the safer, higher-percentage play**.

Once you reach your **corner with the ball**, you have two primary options:

1. **If the opponent is not supersonic and does not pose an immediate threat**, you can **come high over the ball** to **block the inside lane** and maintain control.
2. **If they are charging in supersonic, hit the ball over your own net** (safely across, not into danger), **grab the opposite corner boost**, and **quickly transition into a counterattack**.

By dragging the ball back, I force the opponent to follow me and drain their boost. If they back off, I have a free ball and space.

Going Over You - Hovering

Okay, so we know how to prevent the opponent from pushing through us, and how to deal with grounded and mid-height balls, but how do we deal with opponents going for aerials over the top?

This is where the skill of **hovering** comes in.

Hovering is essentially Rocket League's version of basketball's 'hand in the face'. You are trying to match the **height** of the ball as early as you can so the opponent can see you. This applies whether they are going from the ground or from the wall. The goal is to get up fast and block the ball's height.

Go high early! It is easier to get high and fall down than it is to start at medium height and then try to rise.

The goal with hovering is to do one of two things:

1. If the opponent is going **high** (looking for a double tap), force them even higher by hovering just lower than the ball then boosting upwards into the ball as it comes close, so the angle becomes impossible.
2. If the opponent is going for an **air dribble at mid-height**, force them low by going above the ball and then trying to hit it as you fall, so your 2nd man can take possession easily.

The trick to a hover is that **before you take flight**, you start moving **toward your own net** to generate momentum. Then, when you go up, you are flying **directly upward**. When done correctly, you will slowly drift away from the ball while climbing in height. If you are at the correct height, the opponent, moving faster, will have no choice but to play the ball into you.

Now, as mentioned, you can **force them high or low** depending on their intent. But ideally, you want to **touch the ball** too, ideally towards your corner due to being on a slight inside position. For example, if you want to force them **low,** try to touch the ball **from the top**. If you want to force them **high**, touch it **from below**.

M0nkey M00n, getting ready to hover notice his boost heading backwards and up.

Some tips when hovering:

- Try to **face the opponent** once you are in the air. This makes it easier to control your car, as your inputs will feel more natural.
- You might also want to **approach from a slightly outside shadow** whilst learning. This angle makes it **easier to time your hit** due to your **momentum carrying you into the ball**, and it naturally results in hitting the ball across the pitch, away from danger. While **inside shadows are more optimal** in the long term, they can sometimes lead to **dead balls near your net** or even **own goals** if you are still **mastering aerial control**.

Remember, **hovering is the 1st man's responsibility**, as he is the first line of defence. In the next section, we will cover what the 2nd man should do in these scenarios.

1st Man Defence Conclusion

We now understand that, as the 1st man, our main goal is to protect our 2nd man and control the middle of the field by funnelling opponents toward the corner. By doing this, we can **draw them into low-percentage challenges** and create strong opportunities for counterattacks.

Throughout this chapter, we have covered a range of high-level defensive tools that allow the 1st man to stay composed, unpredictable, and in control. These include:

- **Perfect side flips** to deflect pressure and force awkward plays.
- **Inside shadowing** to funnel plays safely toward the corner.
- **Triangle defending** when you have a boost advantage and want to force the ball centrally for a fast break.
- **Defending from behind**, using pressure to force errors even after being beaten.
- **Snaking**, a powerful fake strategy to break down controlled plays.
- **Hovering**, the essential technique for shutting down aerial plays early.
- And finally, the use of **front-end aggression** to ensure you are pressuring the ball assertively when it is your turn.

When used together, these skills form a complete first-man toolkit within The Pacifist System, allowing you to **slow down the game, take control of possession**, and **set up your teammate for success**.

The 1st man does not dive, does not panic, and does not look for hero plays. They create pressure through presence, guide the play with purpose, and trust the system to do the rest.

DEFENCE - 2ND MAN

The 2nd man is arguably the most important role in the game when it comes to ranking up. If you are attempting to use the advice in this book without a teammate, it will be difficult, as you will be paired with a wide variety of teammates and opponents. However, by forcing yourself into the 2nd man role and applying the information that follows, you should begin to see rank success, even in solo queue.

In Rocket League, the 2nd man is often described as the second player to hit the ball. I define it differently, the 2nd man is **the last man back**, or the player furthest away from the action on your team.

In the following chapter, we will cover how the 2nd man should approach defence and what their main objectives are.

Deep Net Position

One of the most common pieces of incorrect advice is: "*Never end up in your net.*" This could not be further from the truth, especially when done correctly and at the right time. Obviously, if you sit in net all game, you will get heavily destroyed. And equally, if you are allowing opponents to take the middle while sitting in net, your chance of saving a shot is extremely low.

However, that is not how we play this.

It is 2s, and we have a teammate, our 1st man, protecting us from middle attacks and trying to force the ball into the corner. As 2nd man, we will also act as a further, deeper shadow (covered shortly). But for now, when the ball is played into our corners, we **absolutely** want to be in the deep net position.

It is important **not** to be on the curved part of the goal, and instead to be slightly **behind the goal line**. The idea is that when the ball is played from the corner towards the net, the 2nd man is in position to either get a strong clear or take possession for a counterattack.

Being deep in net offers several benefits:

1. **Vision** – As 2nd man, you want to locate the opponent's 2nd man. This helps inform your next move:
    - **Close 2nd man** – Try to intercept the ball or touch it before they do. If they dive, you may have an open net.
    - **Far 2nd man** – Take your time, gather possession, and set up a high-percentage play like a bounce dribble power shot.
    - **Middle or following their teammate into the corner (most common)** – Shoot on net and push hard.
2. **A path to victory** – Your car should be facing 50% toward the play and 50% toward the opponent's net, right in between. This lets you deal with most attacks effectively.
3. **Ability to dodge demos** – You are not locked into a tight position, so you can easily side flip in either direction to dodge a demo and potentially win the ball.
4. **Clarity for your 1st man** – Oddly enough, this is a big one. When your teammate knows you are not going to drive into the corner to bump them or snatch possession, they can confidently make a play, knowing you are behind as backup.

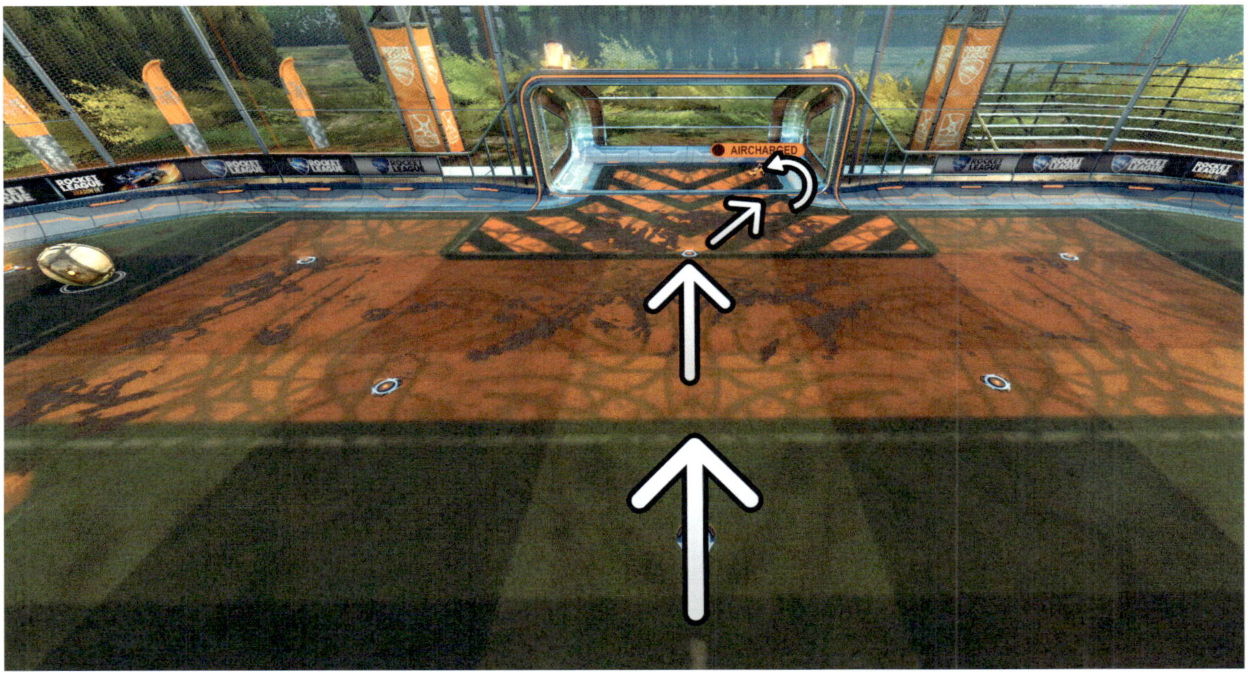

The most effective way to swing into the net, away, then towards.

Rotation tip: When rotating back, ideally, approach down the middle, then turn away from the side the ball is on, enter the net, and power slide to turn and face the play from the opposite deep net position.

Counterattack

The counterattack is the foundation of this system. Our primary goal is to create counterattacks and 2v1s.

To do this effectively as 2nd man, we aim to **control the middle of the field** while far shadowing. Once the opponents get funnelled into the corner, we are already anticipating the counterattack.

As 2nd man, swing into the **deep net position** on the opposite side of the play, and visually hunt for the opponent's 2nd man. As mentioned earlier, what you do next depends entirely on their positioning.

Using my camera to track the 2nd man, I notice they are in no mans land.

Once the ball is forced into the middle, **that is your moment**, take the shot.
From there, immediately transition into offence. Use your momentum to grab their boost and keep the pressure on. The goal is to trap them in a vulnerable spot where they must defend while being starved, opening up more space for your team.

There are some excellent drills to focus on counterattacks, depending on how many players you have in the drills section at the back of the book.

After the initial counterattack is made, we are pushing up fast, as is our previous 1st man (now the 2nd man). The idea is to get **the furthest part of 2nd mans car in front of the opponent's last man.**

Second man is in no mans land (they cannot challenge, or save) so we can shoot on net.

The goal is to **move this line forward as much and as quickly as we can get away with**. Obviously, if we push too far, we will end up side-by-side at the opponent's net with no space to manoeuvre. But ideally, by holding this line just right, we **create fear and panic** in the trailing defender, who is often forced to rush straight to net and will likely miss boost pads in the process.

While this is happening, after we shoot our shot from the net and push up field, we are looking to **bump or demo** the only relevant defender. Whether we connect or not, we will **curve around to their corner boost** right after. Remember not to force a demo in a way that will leave you stuck in the opponent's net.

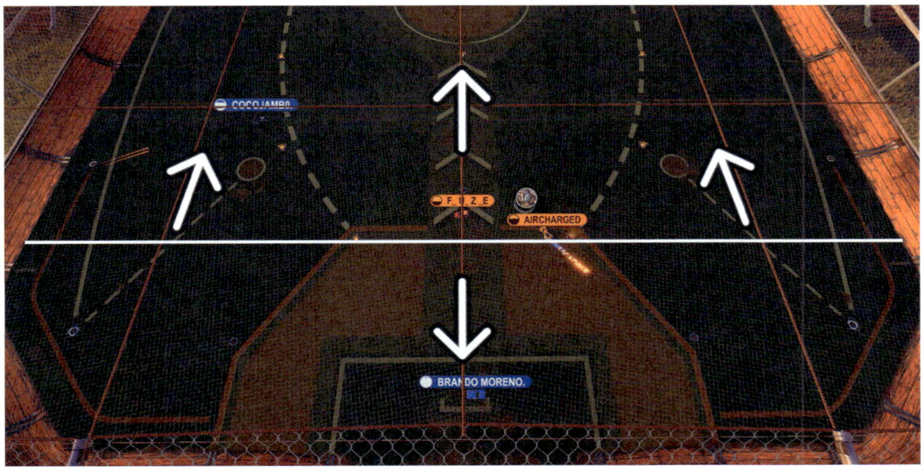

Pushing the 2v1 line up as quick as possible, to keep Brando isolated behind the play.

I often tier boosts as follows:

1. **Tier 1** – Your corner boost
2. **Tier 2** – The mid boost
3. **Tier 3** – The opponent's corner boost

Tiers of each boost.

By stealing the opponent's corner boost, and if we are really sneaky, maybe the mid boost too, we can **trap them in defence with 0 boost**. That now puts us into **Offensive Offence (OO)**, where we can look for the cool stuff coming up later, like Pacifist Pivots, or just keep lifting the ball high until we find a gap.

If at any point the attack does not materialise how we hoped, we can drop back into **Offensive Defence (OD)** or take the ball with us (**Drag back**) and **reset for another counterattack**.

Keep this in mind, **although we love counterattacks, 2v1s, and stealing map space, we do not want to defend for no reason**. A common early mistake with this system is to force yourself into a defensive mindset **even when the opponents are already completely starved** and you have a golden scoring opportunity.

In other words, do not default to shadowing when you are in control. Shadowing is fine **when needed**, but if you are shadowing, it means **the opponent still owns the ball**. And if that is the case, you have lost possession and now must work for a new counter.

So, remember, **keep the attack going**. If it is not working, fine, take it back and try again. But do not surrender pressure for free.

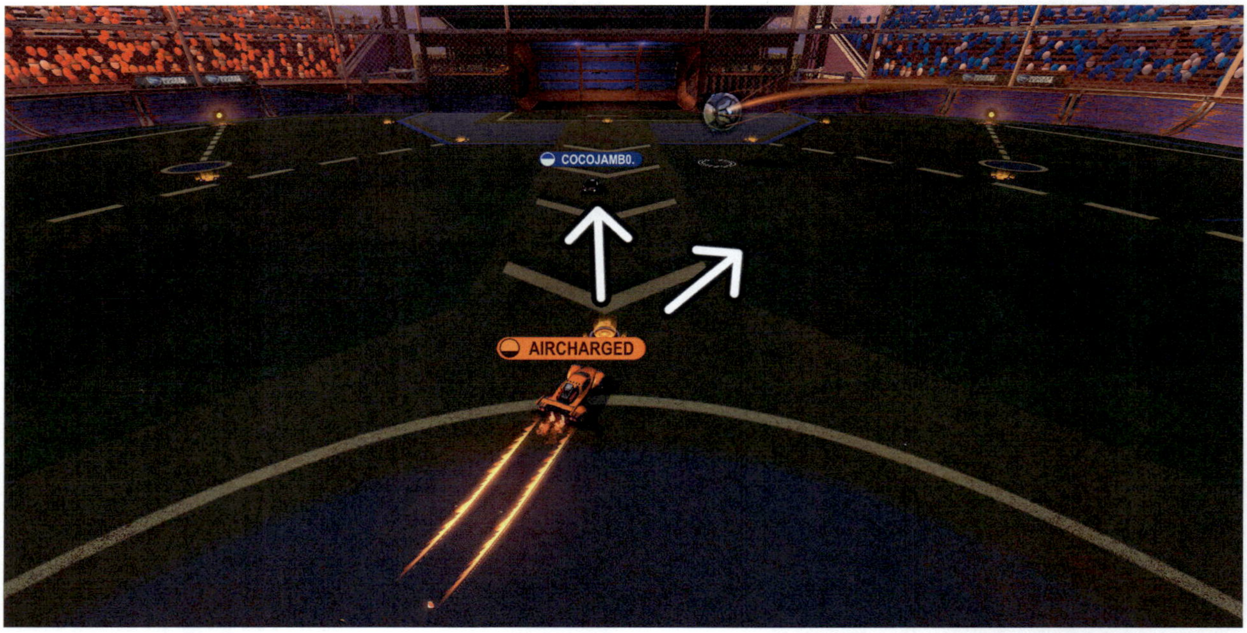

Even though I know I have scored. I am still thinking about either demoing the opponent, or going to the big boost if it gets saved to the side I think it will. Never give up on the play.

Central Build Up / Back Off

As the 2nd man, you are stuck on the central track like a train, think **Thomas the Tank Engine** chugging up and down, living the dream. Your goal is to **continually grab small pads** so you can maintain your central line and stay rock solid in position.

This is crucial because you want to **leave the big boosts for your teammate**, the 1st man. That way, they can pull the ball back, take the big boosts, and strand the opponents in tricky situations with no boost. Not only that, if they are shadowing and defending, funnelling into the corner, they will naturally be closer to our net than the opponent, meaning they can scoop the big boosts as they defend.

When building up on a non-counterattack, such as when your teammate has flicked past the 1st man or forced both opponents to back off, your job is to **build up to pad 1**.

Pad 1 is the **boost pad just before the halfway line**. It is a perfect staging area because it lets you react to multiple outcomes. If your 1st man gets deeper into the opponent's half and it is clear the opponents are struggling to defend, you can push up to **pad 2**, the small pad in the middle just after the halfway line. This is typically where you sit when **you are looking to finish the play**.

And just like before, if a good chance does not come, **be ready to back off,** straight back down the middle line.

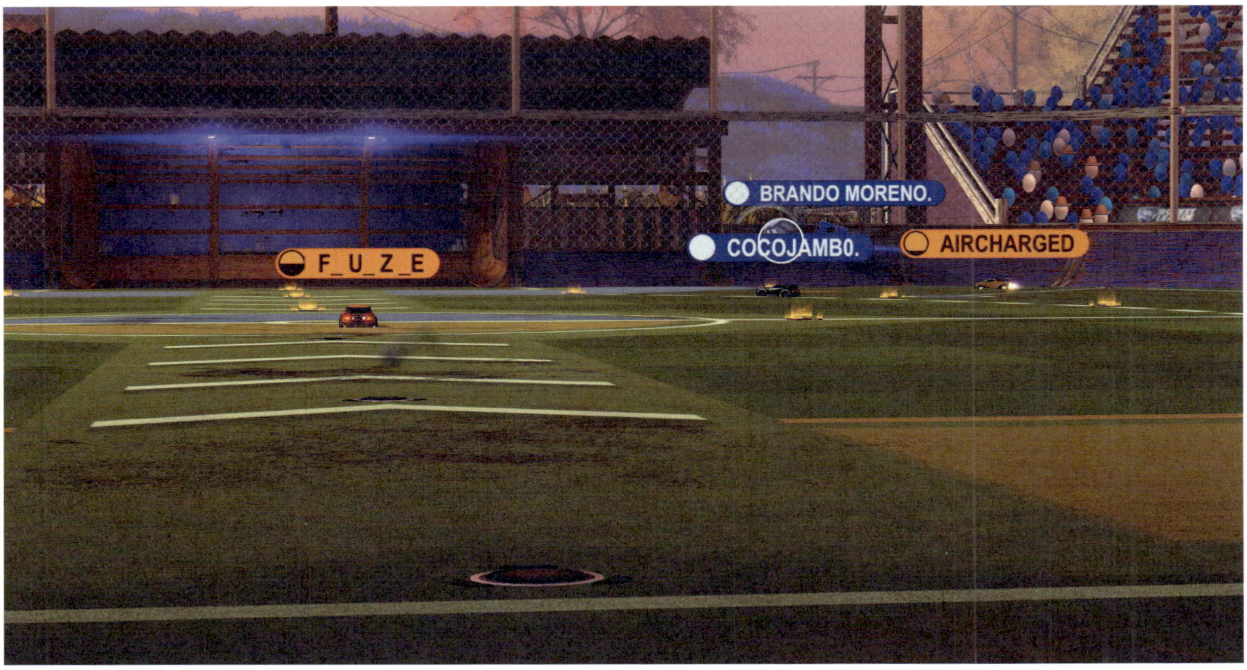

F_U_Z_E going directly down the middle for an easy 36-60 boost.

2nd Man Shadow

When driving down the middle in Offensive Defence (OD), you become a **2nd man shadower.** You are not shadowing the **ball** directly here, you are more so **shadowing your teammate**. This ensures you will not bump into them or crowd their space. As they move back, **you also need to move back**, creating the room they need to make their play.

The goal of this setup is to have your **1st man push the opponents away from the centre**, staying close to the play, shadowing before no-man's land. Meanwhile, as 2nd man, you want to be **shadowing far**, after no-man's land. This creates a layered defence.

That way, if the opponent tries to dribble or set up a shot, the **1st man** can use a **perfect side flip** to put the ball into the corner. And if they do get a shot off, **you**, as the 2nd man shadowing further away, can **do the exact same**, jump up and side flip into the ball to send it into the corner, when this happens your momentum will move with the ball, also putting you in the corner, you will now be the **1st man**.

In situations where the ball is higher, you may need to **double jump** to reach it, but the idea stays the same, protect the centre and buy time.

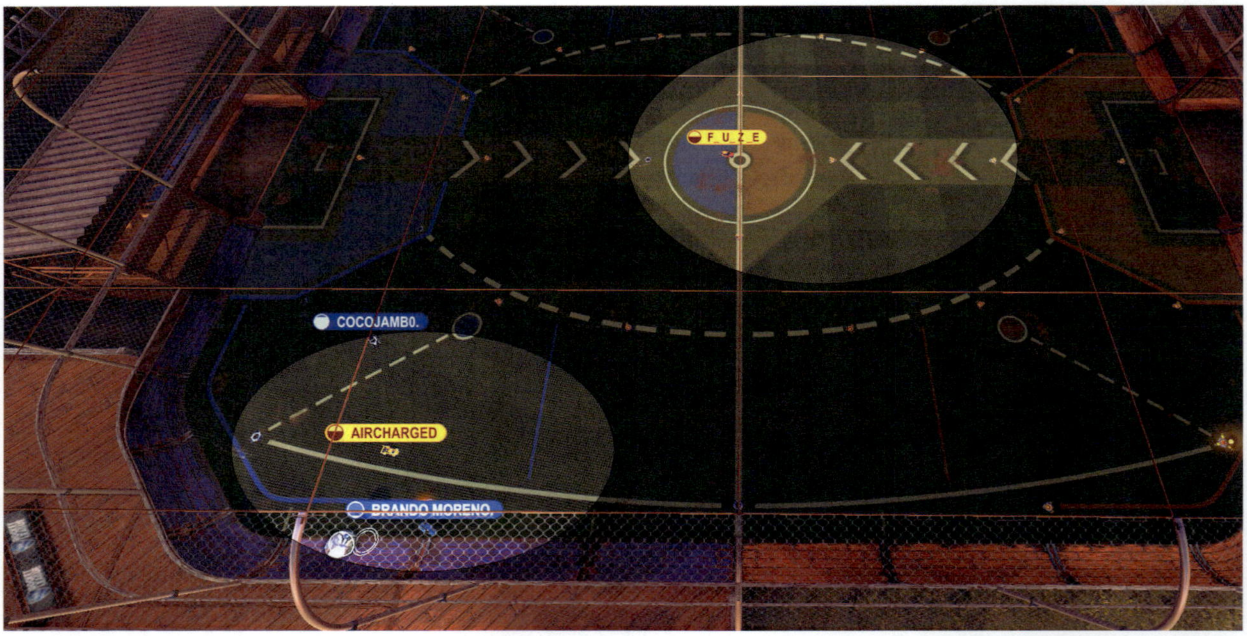

*Each player should be defending a different area. For example I am defending **before** no man's land. And F_U_Z_E is defending **after** no man's land. This way, I can prevent control, and he can prevent shots on net with easy saves.*

Early Or Late

This is a key decision-making tool for the 2nd man when defending alone against an attack that is going towards the corner, or coming from the deep wing. If the ball is coming down the wing (not directly toward net), you must instantly assess your timing and decide whether you are **early or late**.

If you are **early**, you can rotate into **deep net** and set up properly before the shot is taken. From there, you can defend in the **Pacifist** manner and look for a counterattack.

If you are **late**, you will not reach the deep net position before the shot comes in. In this case, you must **remain outside the net**, facing the net. From this position, you attempt to **intercept or block the shot**. If the shot is aimed at the **backboard**, your goal is to challenge either **before, during**, or **immediately after** the ball makes contact with the board to prevent a follow-up or double tap.

However, try to **avoid doing this when the opponent is attacking directly to net**, as they have too many options, if **they are attacking directly to net, even if you are early, do not go into the net** as shadow saving is much more effective in this situation.

As I am late to get into net, and because the opponent is attacking the net directly. I can easily shadow save this to the corner, either for my teammate, or myself to take.

As the opponents went to the corner, and I was early to position, I can come from a deep net position for a counterattack.

Trigger

Early on, when players are learning The Pacifist System, I like to use the **small boost pad** on the **side-line between the big mid boost and the back boost** as a **trigger**. When the ball moves past that pad, the **2nd man** should immediately rotate into the **deep net position**.

As the ball comes across the trigger pad, F_U_Z_E will instantly go into deep net ready for the counterattack.

If done correctly, your defence will now be **primed and ready to counter**.

As you get better at the game, you will be able to read plays much earlier, and will not need to rely on the trigger as heavily. For example, if the ball is cleared into your corner, you can already begin moving into net **before** it even reaches the trigger pad.

As I have played this system so much, I already know what is about to happen, so I am already set in deep net position before the trigger pad has been hit.

Hybrid Shadow

This is used a lot in higher ranks and especially in solo queue. It comes into play when your 1st man has overcommitted, usually by forcing the offence with 0 boost or diving into the opponent's corner. In these situations, you cannot simply back off and sit in net, as you are pretty much guaranteed to get scored on due to being locked into position.

Remember, the reason **deep net** works so well is because the 1st man is controlling the middle of the map and funnelling the ball into low-percentage angles that are easier to save. Defending the ball head-on, however, is really rough.

To avoid this, we go into a **hybrid shadow** when we are all alone. The trick here is to stay just on the edge of no-man's land, as we are unable to get into a close shadow (if we tried they could just shoot over us). So instead, we move slightly off the centre line, to the side closest to the ball, but only just (around two car lengths).

From there, attempt an **inside** or **inline shadow**. You can even move into an **outside shadow** if it seems appropriate.

It is important to note, this **inability to move smoothly from far shadow to close shadow** is one of the key reasons why the standard way of playing Rocket League is outdated. For example, if you are facing forward and approaching the ball as 2nd man, and the opponent shoots, it is often a guaranteed goal as you are too wide, too close and not goal side. Rotation-based systems continually create gaps that a good offensive player will easily exploit.

In this situation my teammate has overcommit and left me in a 2v1. As 2nd man, I will move off the centre line slightly. This allows me to defend with the balls path towards my net. This is also great for timewasting and allows my teammate to come back and defend from behind.

Common Team Position

This is worth mentioning as it happens frequently.

If the ball is in your **corner** with **1st man** close to the play and the ball spills **centre**, the opponents could have their **2nd man** waiting in the middle for a shot. In this scenario:

- The **1st man** stays on the **backboard** to prevent a **double tap** or **aerial** attempt.
- The **2nd man**, who is positioned **deep in net**, **chases out** and dives on the ball. Or, if the opponent is able to jab the ball over the 2nd man before they are able to dive on the ball, then aim to bump/ demo or jump and bump/ demo the player who jabbed the ball.

The reason this **dive** is safe is because the resulting play becomes a **1st man vs 2nd man** scenario, **your 1st man vs their 2nd man**. That is a favourable match-up when executed correctly.

As soon as the ball leaks out, as 2nd man it is important to go directly to the ball as quick as possible and aim to take possession or 50/50 the opponents last man.

2nd Man Defence Conclusion

Being 2nd man is not about being passive, it is about being **prepared**.

While the first man tests the opponent and creates openings, it is the second man who truly decides the outcome of the play. When you are disciplined, patient, and smart in this role, you are not just reacting, you are **controlling the game from the shadows**.

Mastering 2nd man means:

- **Choosing patience over panic**.
- **Positioning with purpose, not just presence**.
- **Playing the long game**, knowing that the ball will come to you, and when it does, you will be ready.

In The Pacifist System, we do not gamble on pressure. We **earn possession through positioning**, and the second man is the backbone of that philosophy.

OFFENCE - 1ST MAN

The fun stuff.

I started this book with **defence** because I believe it is more important than **offence**, especially for ranks **GC and under**, where most goals come easily with solid defending.

However, one thing that has become clear from teaching this system for the past **4 years** is this, some players will have ball **possession**, could start an **attack**, but instead **give it away** just to go back into defence.

Let me be absolutely clear, **if we have possession, our goal has already been met**. The next step is to put **quality pressure** on the opponents. That means:

- **Collapsing the defence** (forcing both defenders into bad positions, like moving away from the ball or getting stuck in net).
- **Separating the defenders**, or
- **Causing double commits.**

These are all fairly easy to achieve and often happen automatically if you follow a few **simple principles**.

So again, **this is a counterattack system**. Once you can **attack, you attack**. If you **own the ball, you attack**. Do **not** give the ball away repeatedly just so you can return to defence. While that kind of discipline is powerful, it causes you to **lose pressure, lose your advantage,** and ultimately **lose respect** from your opponent.

As much as I love **defence**, the purpose of our system is to **quickly shut down attacks**, then **turn the tables** and force the opponent to defend our offence.

And remember, **on attack, put the ball high**. This:

- **Blinds the opponent** (they are forced to look up).
- **Causes panic.**
- **Burns their boost.**
- **Prevents easy control or clearances.**

Lateral Dribble

The **lateral dribble** is the ultimate starting weapon for offence, but it requires a solid understanding of both **your goals** and the **opponent's**.

The initial lateral dribble position is actually a **weak one**. You are placing yourself on the **outside of the ball**, which means that if the opponent challenges with a 50/50, you are in a bad position to win it.

This is why you should **only go for a lateral dribble if you have space** to execute it.
If the opponent is **close enough to challenge** before you get the dribble going, **do not do it!**

In that case, stay on the **inside** of the ball and look to use **single jump 50s, fadeaway 50s**, or **side flip 50s** (covered next).

However, if you **do** have space for the lateral dribble, your goal is to **smoothly push the ball** from one side of the pitch to the other. Ideally, keep the ball **flat and grounded**, bounce adds difficulty in both **control** and **vision**.

During the dribble:

- Be **active with your camera usage**, switching between **car cam** and **ball cam** to stay aware of your opponent.
- How wide your lateral movement is should depend on your goal. Going wider is more difficult but gives more space. Going narrower attacks quicker, but can create less space. But to start with, I recommend aiming toward the **opponent's opposite-side trigger boost.**

Now, let's say the opponent **does challenge** during your lateral dribble.
You have three core **50/50** techniques to stay in control and come out ahead.

In this position, the opponent was too close to go for a lateral dribble, so I waited and took a low 50/50 from the inside position, this game me a free ball.

50/50s

If you did not know, a **50/50** is when two players hit or challenge the ball at roughly the same time. They are called 50/50s because it is estimated you will win 50% and lose 50% of them.

But here, we like to call them 90/10s, because we aim for a 90%-win rate.

Low 50s in the corner on the inside are so powerful, here I use a low 50 as the opponent is too close for me to use a lateral dribble.

The Single Jump 50

The first and most common 50 is the **single jump 50**. As the opponent comes in, you simply jump and block their hit. In a **lateral dribble**, you are already in control, and importantly, you should only be going for a lateral dribble if the opponent is on the **same side** as you or **central**.
We rarely, if ever, want to lateral dribble **into** an opponent who is on the **opposite side**, as that creates no space and kills the play.

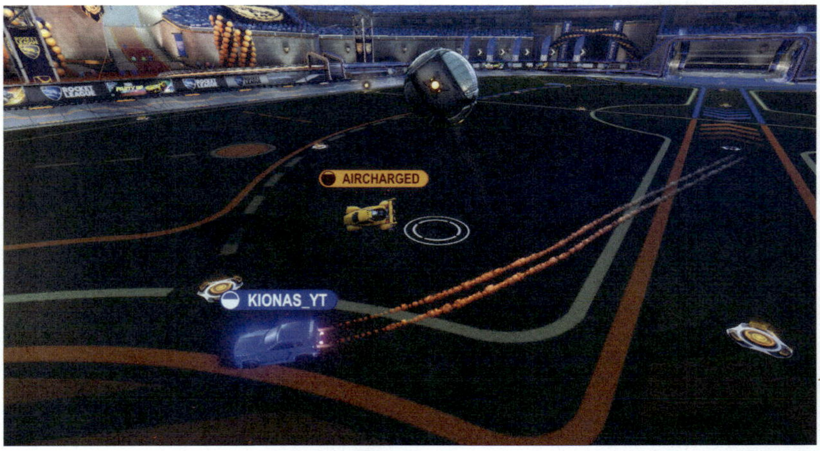

Winning a low 50 from a lateral dribble from an opponent attempting a jab.

With the lateral dribble, you are **side-on** to the ball, which gives you a **huge hitbox**. If the opponent challenges head-on, they are very unlikely to win.

And even if they do 'win', the ball will usually end up in your **corner**, which, in this system, is your safe space anyway.

To perform a **single jump 50**, simply time a jump when the opponent dives in:

- Try not to hold the jump too long, jumping too high can lift you off the ball.
- Aim to hit the **middle** of the ball in height.

Strengths:

- Very safe.
- Strong if timed well.

Weaknesses:

- If the opponent is **very close** and does not dive, they may sneak the ball or trip you on landing.
- If they are **supersonic** and speed flip perfectly, you may get **pushed back** or even **demoed**.

Lateral dribble creates such a strong hitbox for a 50/50.

Fadeaway 50

The **fadeaway 50** was inspired by the great **oKhalid**. When an opponent is extremely close, the first to dodge is usually in the weaker position, as they are locked into their animation and easier to read.

So, if you are **dribbling** (especially lateral or wing dribbling) and the opponent is close and **flipping a lot**, this is your go-to.

The **fadeaway** absorbs the opponent's momentum and takes the ball to safety.
Done right, it can **kill the ball**, sending the opponent flying **past** it and giving you **free possession**.

To perform a fadeaway 50:

- As the opponent dives in, **turn away** (usually toward the inside).
- The ball will hit the **mid/back** of your car and go safe.
- If you 'lose', it still goes to the corner, no problem, you just reset.

Be very cautious when using the fadeaway 50/50, as if it is performed late, as in when the ball is already beyond the centre of the map, or near it, the ball could go to net if done incorrectly.

Fadeaway 50: Turning away on the opponents challenge to regather the ball after.

Weaknesses:

- If the opponent **jabs** the ball instead of diving, it can go **over** your car
- You could get **demoed** if they keep driving through. To counter this, mix in **single jump 50s** or **save your dodge** to recover.

Side Flip 50

The **side flip 50** is incredibly powerful, especially as you move up the ranks. It becomes the **go-to** method for dealing with **speed flips** and **supersonic challenges**.

With a **single jump**, you have no momentum pushing you forward.
But with a **side flip**, the animation launches you into the ball, which gives you a chance to **nullify** their challenge or even win it outright.

It also gives you a **huge hitbox**, just like with the single jump.

Weaknesses:

- If the opponent **fakes**, you are flipping the ball **away** from yourself.
- You are also **committing**, so recovery becomes harder.

This is why many players, including myself, tend to try and mix them as much as possible, personally, I use fade aways a lot, and I use a single jump, that will become a side flip once the opponent touches the ball.

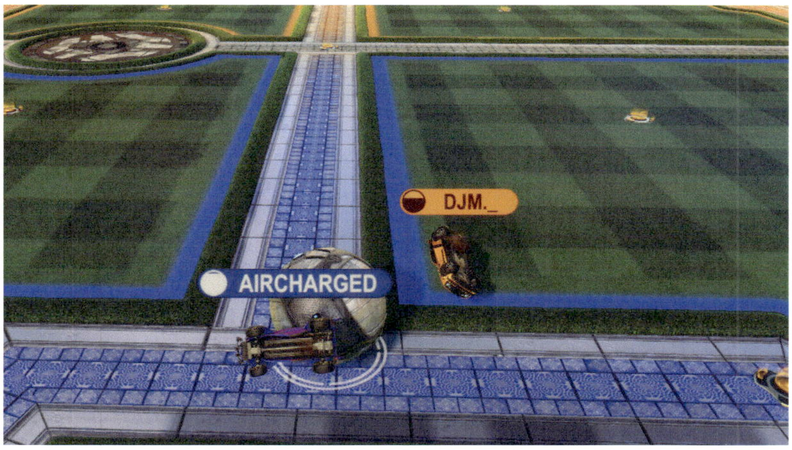

Using a side flip 50/50 to neutralise the opponents dive.

Recap:

If you are lateral dribbling and you are going to get challenged:

1. Get to a **goal side / inside** position.
2. Choose your 50 technique:
    - Use **single jump 50s** when you see the opponent diving, or drive challenging.
    - Use **fadeaway 50s** when the opponent is extremely close.
    - Use **side flip 50s** when you are being speed flipped or challenged at high speed.

Mastering these is how we turn '50/50s' into '**90/10s**'.

Outplays

Ok so, what if you are actually able to create?

Well first, remember, even taking a **high percentage 50/50** is a form of creating. But if we are given **space**, then it is **show time!**

With most outplays, just like with 50s, what we go for depends on what the **opponent shows us**. Over time, and with practice, you will get better and better at selecting the **highest percentage outplay** in any given situation.

The first, most classic outplay and finisher is the **hook shot**.

The Hook Shot

The first instructional video I ever made focused on this exact shot, it is also the starting point of my free online Rocket League belt path course.

The hook shot is perfect when both defenders have been forced to back off fully on the **same wing** you are starting from, or if one defender has been demoed while the other retreats. Essentially, it is a great **go-to** when you have been given space and there is **no one defending the far side** of the pitch.

Setting up an unsaveable hook shot.

To perform a hook shot:

1. Begin pushing the ball towards the opponents **trigger pad** (the pad between big mid boost, and the opponents big back boost).
2. Try not to use much boost, a firm, controlled push is ideal.
3. Then **kick your car out and turn into the ball** (without drifting), using boost **on the moment of contact**.
4. The trick is to pad effectively as you move into the shot and avoid wasting boost too early.
5. You ideally want to **reach supersonic right as you strike the ball**.

For further help, head to YouTube and type in "AirCharged hook shot pink", or scan the QR code next to the title for a video with a training pack to help.

How To Power Slide

Before we go into the next section, I think it is important to cover how to actually power slide and turn in general.

Learning to turn well is one of the most underrated mechanics in the game. Everyone knows how to boost and flip, but turning is what gives you the options in the first place. If you cannot turn efficiently, you are going to feel sluggish, overshoot plays, or spin out when the pressure hits.

Here is the first thing, **driving slower gives you a tighter turning radius**. Sounds obvious, but most players do not do it, they boost around and try to power slide everything. Instead, **ease off the throttle** and let the car wrap around naturally. The tighter you need the turn, the more you should slow down.

The **power slide** is a brilliant tool, but only when used with control. If you spam it too early or too late, you will slide out wide or spin completely. Instead, start your turn first, then **tap power slide** just as the turn begins to tighten. It is important to also finish the turn without any power slide whilst accelerating (even if that is slowly) to create a nice, sharp but smooth turn.

Do not be afraid to **use brake taps** either, they are great for quick pivots and tight turns when boost would send you flying wide.

Quick Tips:

- **Drive slower for tighter turns.**
- **Boost widens turns**, feather it or drop it entirely when turning.
- **Power slide after the turn starts**, not before.
- **Finish the turn without power slide.**
- Use brake taps to control oversteer or pivot sharply where required.
- If you're missing 50s or overshooting shadows, it is probably your turning.

The Power Slide Cut

The power slide cut is an excellent move when the opponent has given you space but may still challenge quickly, either because they have not fully backed off, or they are looking for a quick interception. It is also great as a variation in offence when you want to keep your approach unpredictable.

A key tip, **always use power slide cuts proactively**.

Do not try to 'time' the opponent's challenge, there are too many variables. If you suspect they will dive in, just commit and cut instantly. However, if they clearly back off, you can take your time and use the cut to set up a bounce dribble, a carry, or other attacking options.

To perform a power slide cut:

1. Visualise two sets of train tracks, one for your car and one for the ball.
2. The tracks should be spaced by about the width of a car.
3. Push the ball onto its track, then peel off onto your own track and accelerate to slightly overtake the ball.
4. Once you are ahead of the ball, **power slide turn into it**, if done correctly, your front wheels (not the front of the car) will make contact and cut the ball.

You can tweak the timing to vary the outcome, a quicker cut gives more of an angle, while a slightly delayed one adds lift. Use the QR code by the title for a video example.

Now that we have covered proactive power slide cuts, let's explore what options are available once you have got the ball bouncing.

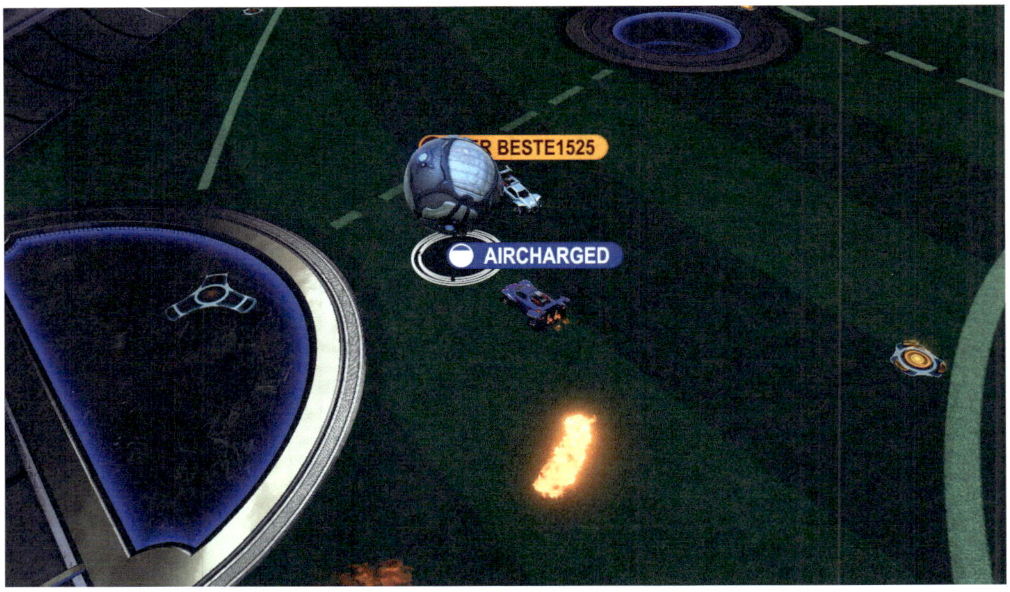

The power slide cut done early is extremely powerful as few expect it.

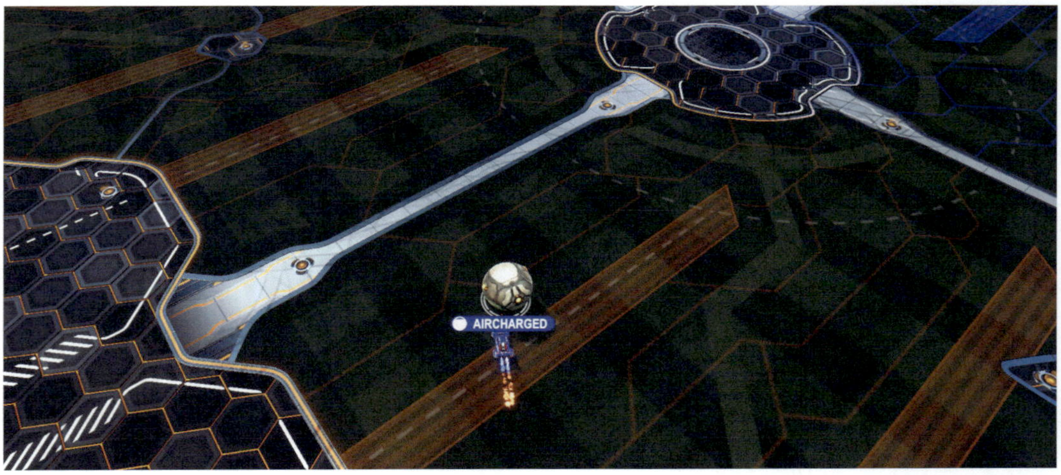

Step 1: Push the ball in a lateral manner.

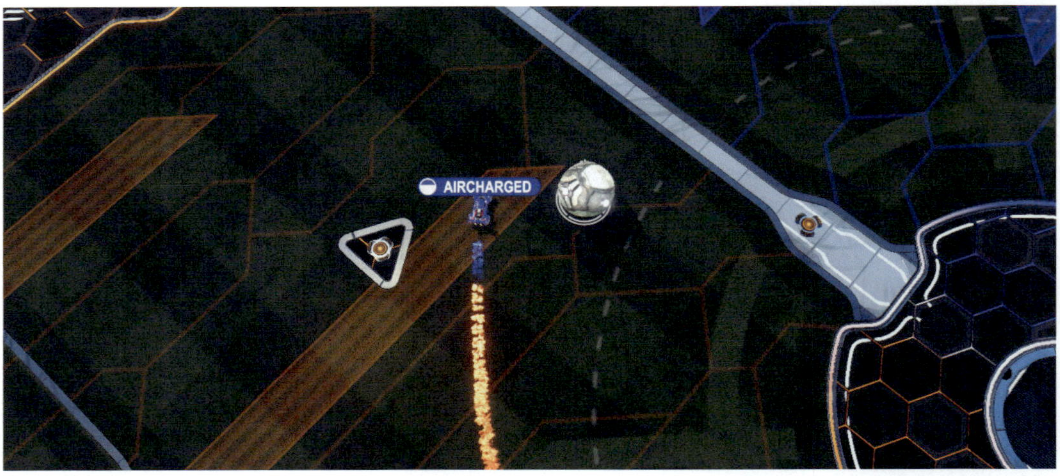

Step 2 : Move in the same direction as the ball, but on a path slightly to the side of it.

Step 3: Use power slide and turn into the ball to hit it on the same area as the front wheel.

Instant Outplays

Instant outplays can come from a natural bounce, a carry, or be set up through a **power slide cut**, or even something as simple as a jab off the wall. One thing to keep in mind is that if you already have a nice bounce or flick available, you **do not** need to go into a lateral dribble first (although moving into space with one can be useful).

In fact, I have found that **attacking as soon as possible**, directly around or over the opponent, tends to be more effective. This prevents them from getting comfortable or settling into a defensive rhythm. However, I should just mention, this can become predictable, even if it is effective. So, if that begins to not work, go back to lateral dribbles to create angles.

The Instant Flick

The instant flick is a hybrid move, sitting right between a shot and a flick. It is also known as a **tail whip flick**. What makes this move so powerful is that there is **no setup** required. If the ball has a bounce and you are nearby, you can pull it off instantly.

This move becomes **overpowered** around Grand Champion rank due to how many players dive. Being able to instantly launch the ball into the air not only sets up your offence but also blinds the opponent, as the rising ball breaks their vision of your car.

To perform it, position yourself **just inside** the circle that appears beneath the ball when it is in the air. **Hold jump** to get more height, then follow with a **front flip**. As you improve, you can progress to a **diagonal flip**, which raises one corner of your car even higher and makes your flicks much tougher to read and deal with.

The instant flick is one of my favourite out plays against a last man.

Flicks

Aside from the instant flick, we of course can carry flick too. This can be done from **any kind of carry**, it does not require a lateral dribble. Simply carry the ball on your car, then use the appropriate dodge depending on the ball's position.

- If the ball is **forward** on your car, go for a front flip.
- If it is off to either side, **flip to that side**.

There is not a huge amount to say about flicks here, **most players already know everything they need** to.

However, if you do want further detail, I have a **full Flick Mastery guide** on my YouTube channel, which shows **each flick** and the tier it belongs in. Use the QR code to open the video playlist.

The 45 degree flick, one of the most powerful flicks.

Under Cut

The **under cut** is an excellent technique for achieving fast outplays in the corner, particularly against overly aggressive opponents. While it is often safe to absorb a 50/50 in the corner, knowing the second man can clean up and counter, it is even better to take control and create a 2v1 situation on **your terms**.

That is where the under cut shines.

As the name suggests, this move involves cutting beneath the ball. Corners are the ideal environment for this due to their shape and the ball's tendency to roll down the wall or drop from the backboard. When the ball is coming down in the corner, instead of waiting for a 50/50, you can **pre-emptively** boost underneath it. The key is to approach slightly lower than the ball, momentarily slow down to line up your cut, then sharply turn and boost through the underside of the ball.

When done correctly, this hits the bottom of the ball, lifting it over the challenging opponent and giving you clear space to continue the play, often turning defence into immediate offence.

Using the under cut for a quick outplay.

Jabs

Jabs, jabs, jabs. I love them! Keep in mind that our main goal on offence is to get the ball high, not just fire off shots that roll in low. And that is why the jab is the ultimate move.

Every play realistically starts with a jab. When you move the ball forward, you are using micro jabs. But the ones I am really talking about here are the **high jabs**, the ones that lift the ball into the air and **start your offence properly**.

Jabbing the backboard is one of my favourites, but honestly, jabbing or even **hook shots off the wall** are incredible too, they are great for creating high balls that let you go on the attack with control.

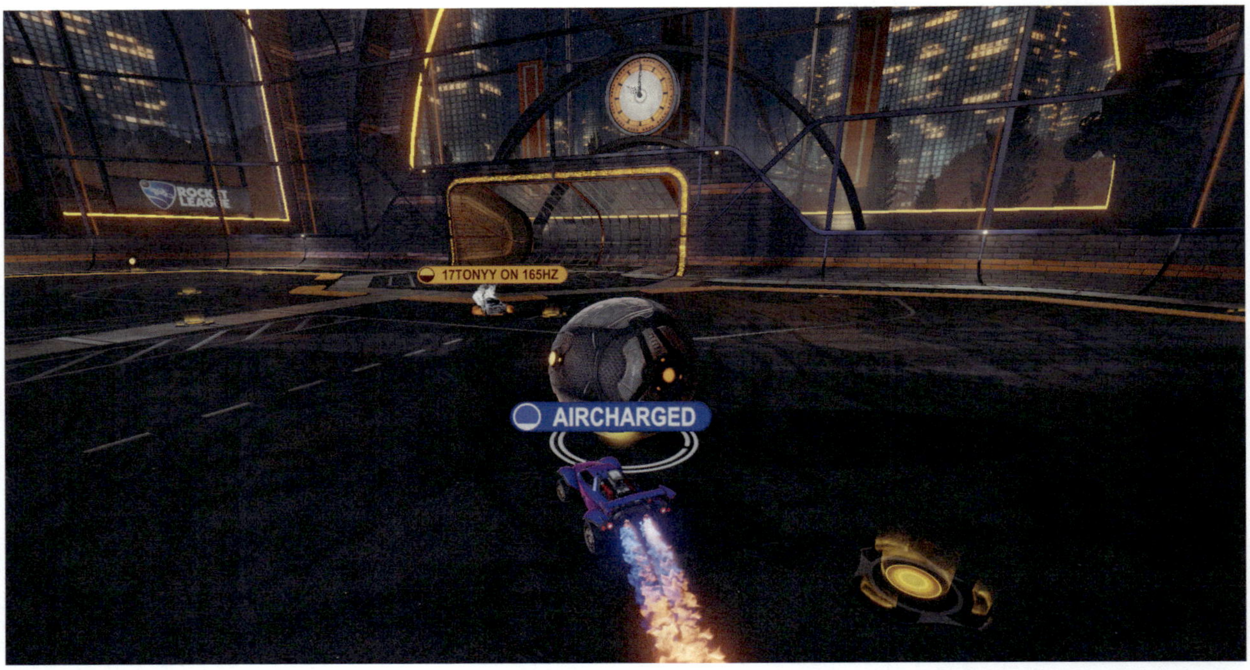

Using a jab is a great idea when the opponent is being aggressive as they often displace from the net quickly.

Quick tip: When you are about to shoot and the opponents are sitting in net, **do not shoot it low**, that will go straight to them and be easy to control. Instead, **jab the ball high** and watch them panic!

Bounce Dribble Power Shots

The bounce dribble is perfect for instant, high-threat plays. It is the **most effective dribble in the game**, but also one of the most difficult to master. While it can lead into a wide range of moves, we are focusing here on the **power shot**, the cleanest way to convert a bounce into a goal.

This style was popularised by **oKhalid**, but dates all the way back to **Kuxir97**, with legends like **Squishy, Lachinio**, and **ScrubKilla** all showcasing elite power shots in their prime.

The key to a proper bounce dribble power shot is to **avoid dribbling directly at the net**. Instead, create a **slight angle**. Angles give you options. With the right car positioning and dodge timing, you can aim **anywhere in the goal**, far post, near post, or straight through the keeper.

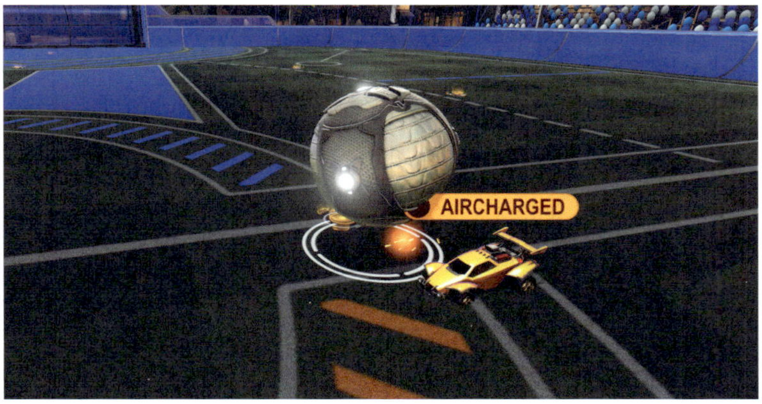

Using an angle with the bounce dribble ensures success, notice where the ball is hitting the car.

To set up the bounce dribble, you usually want to **minimise boost usage** and let the ball bounce naturally. Wrap around the outside of the ball and begin **guiding it toward the net** using soft touches with the **side of your car,** the same zone you would use for a **power slide cut**. As the ball **rises on each bounce**, apply **small redirects** to steer it inward. This keeps your control tight while preparing the angle for a clean shot.

As the ball is rising, I am trying to hit it with the closest corner of the car, this generates the most power on the side flip.

If you strike the ball **on the rise**, use the **inside front corner** of your car to drive it toward the **far post**. If you shoot **as the ball is falling**, try and clip it with the **outside corner** of your car as you side flip through, aiming to target the front post. However, these are my preferences, you can time these however you want.

To hit a clean power shot, **side flip toward the inside**, as your bounce dribble will usually be wrapping around from the outside. As you improve, you can even begin **speed flipping into these shots** in the right moments to maximise power.

These shots also introduce **micro rhythm breaks**, subtle changes in tempo that catch defenders off guard. The ball is being bounced slowly, then suddenly it is launched with power off the bounce at random times. These micro breaks sit within the **macro rhythm break** of The Pacifist System itself. Slow, safe defending that flips instantly into a dangerous counterattack.

To practise bounce dribble power shots, make sure you are striking with the **front corners of the car**. As the ball bounces, time your shot to hit it cleanly with the **inside or outside corner**, depending on the angle and target. Both approaches are deadly. Both take finesse.

As I am hitting this ball as its falling, I am actually hitting it with the opposite corner as my car rolls underneath from the side flip.

Aerials

You may have noticed that I do not mention aerials very much. That is because most players are already obsessed with them. But let me be clear, **aerials are extremely important**, especially as you push beyond Grand Champion.

Now you might be wondering: *"Do I have to wait until GC to start aerialing?"*
Yes and no.

Defensive Aerials

As previously discussed, on **defence**, aerials are necessary much earlier in rank (high plat and above). If the ball is high and threatening, you will need to hover to block it. If you are second man and first man cannot get up in time, you might need to fly out and challenge. These are practical, valuable aerials.

Offensive Aerials

On **offence**, however, things get trickier.

Most players aerial just to hit the ball. It is the airborne version of smashing the ball into the corner without a plan. Even in **GC3**, I still see players launching aerials into the side wall just because they can. That's why I generally advise players to **avoid offensive aerials in-game until around Champ–GC**.
Not because aerials are not useful, but because **you need to learn when they have actual value**.

Here are some aerial plays that **consistently create value**, once you are ready:

- **Basic Air Dribble** – Carry the ball up with control, then **accelerate at the last moment** for a powerful finish.
- **Air Dribble Bump** – Start an air dribble, then fly ahead of the ball and **demo the goalie**.
- **Air Dribble 50** – Glide into the ball while **intentionally pulling your car back** to fill the gap the opponent would otherwise clear into.
- **Double Touches** – Always a strong offensive tool when done cleanly.

These aerials are especially strong in **Offensive Offence (OO)** situations where defenders are already in net with low boost. You want to give them something awkward to deal with.

But on a **pure counterattack**, if the ball is high and you have got space, just get up quickly and **hit the ball on target**. Simple can be deadly.

A simple air dribble is usually more than enough when you are attacking the air. Going for extras such as flip resets can cause more accidents, especially early on.

50s

As mentioned earlier, when we have possession, we want to attack using any of the methods previously mentioned. However, even if we **cannot get a lateral dribble** going, or are struggling to get the ball on our car, if we are on offence and **moving the ball forward**, we can **absolutely take a 50 with the opponent**.

The reason this works is because **we own the ball**, we are already moving it in our favour. So theoretically, we should be able to **push it into a gap** and then **flip through that gap** to break past the opponent.

This is another reason why **diving on a ball as a defender** is often a bad idea, if the offensive player is patient and playing high percentage, they will usually come out ahead.

From a 50/50, if it is a strong win, you will often either want to **instantly finish** the play or **keep your momentum** for a **demo, bump**, or **boost grab** in the nearby areas.

OFFENCE - 2ND MAN

If the **1st man** is the offensive catalyst, then the **2nd man** is the anchor, allowing the team to attack safely and often getting rewarded with the finish.

The key difference between **The Pacifist System** and traditional play is that the 2nd man is not trying to force their way in. If the 1st man is on the ball and attacking, the 2nd man will **gradually build up through the middle**, leaving ample space.

I often recommend following up **down the central line**, around **2–3 boost pads** behind the 1st man. I want you to imagine you're being pulled forward by your teammate, attached by a piece of string. We want that string to stay **tight**.

- If you are **too far back**, the string snaps.
- If you are **too close**, the string goes slack.

This also applies when moving back on defence, we call this '**string theory**'.

When done right, if something goes wrong, the 2nd man can instantly **step in and recover** the play.

Although the 2nd man plays further back compared to standard play, it does not mean they will not have chances to score, in fact, they will often have **more opportunities**, as they can **read the play** and move in with momentum.

And remember, **unless the net is wide open**, that strike should ideally be a **jab to raise the ball high** and pressure the defence.

2nd Man Bursts

The **2nd man burst** happens when the 2nd man is in net, and the 1st man successfully funnels the ball into the corner. Once the ball is played across the net, the 2nd man steps up and **takes the shot**.

As soon as that happens, the 2nd man **bursts forward with the ball**, transitioning into the new **1st man** and **countering as hard as possible**.

The idea is to quickly get a shot towards the net, **collapse the opponents**, and force them to defend against high pressure attacks while you begin **stealing their big boost pads**.

If done correctly, your team can **keep the attack going**, putting the opponents in deeper water until a **very high-percentage** shot opens up.

You will notice there is not a huge section about 2nd man in offence, and that is because their role is to **support the play, get the jab or finish where possible**, and then **rotate into 1st man**.

Switching from 1st to 2nd man after bursting into a counterattack.

OFFENCE - TEAM

One of the great advantages of **The Pacifist System** is that, because players are following a **structured approach** and are **positioned in a consistent and memorable way**, a wide range of **team plays become accessible**.

Even simple ideas, such as **purposely creating a dead 50/50 in the middle against the last man**, often result in a goal, because the **2nd man will already be positioned centrally, ready to finish**.

However, despite the natural effectiveness for **counterattacks and prolonged pressure**, there are two specific moves that are heavily utilised in **The Pacifist System** when on **Offensive Offence (OO)**.

These are used in situations where you are struggling to find space to score, but you know:

- The **opponents are low on boost**, or
- You have **collapsed them into their net** and want to **reduce their chances of saving the ball**.

Even though the opponents have boost. Because we collapsed them, we are expecting to score.

Trailer

This is one of my favourite plays, and often the most common one I use in **GC3 and above** lobbies. The reason? It is **extremely high percentage** and creates **space**, which can be hard to come by at higher ranks.

A **trailer play** is done when the **1st man**, who has possession, deliberately moves the ball into a position that puts it **closer to their teammate than the opponent**. They then continue to **push forward, curving off the ball** to **bump or demo the defender**.

This can be **so effective** that you can even bump **both defenders**, leaving your teammate with an **open net**.

If, for any reason, the 1st man **does not manage to land the demo**, they can **rotate out**, and the **2nd man** (now on the ball) can take a **safe 50** if needed.

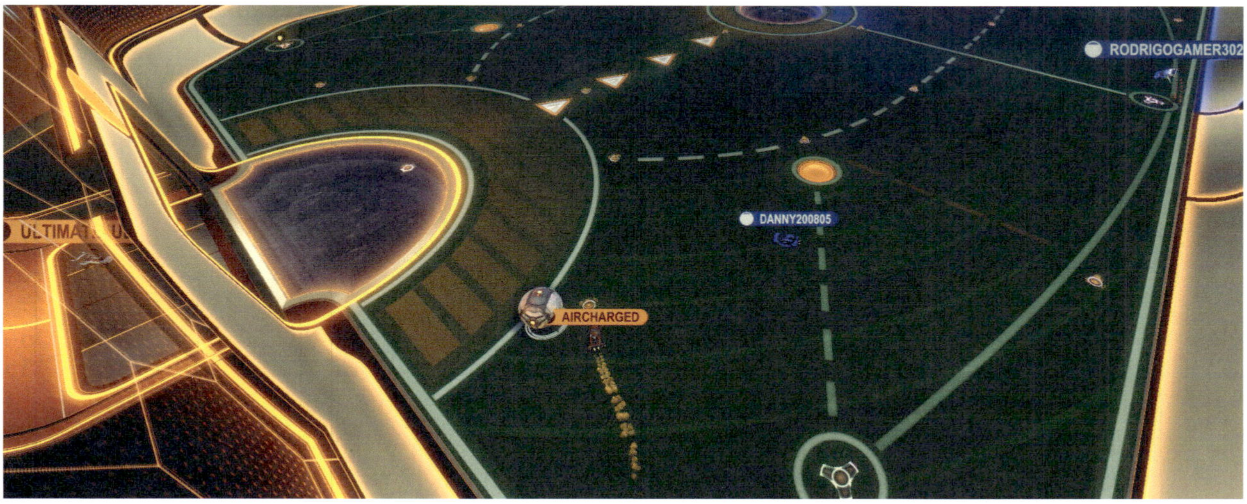

Trailer 1: Pushing the ball toward teammate ready to peal off.

Trailer 2: As soon as you peal, go for a bump or demo on the nearest player.

Trailer 3: 2nd man pushes directly at net, 1st man goes for a bump on the opponents 2nd man.

Trailer 4: Goal.

The Pacifist Pivot

The **original play**. The Pacifist Pivot differs from the **Trailer** in that it is a **back pass or drag back play**, rather than a hand-off moving forward.

With a pivot, the **1st man**, who is in the opponent's corner with the ball, will **wrap around the ball** and play it **backwards towards the 2nd man,** who is waiting near **pad 1 or pad 2**.

The **2nd man** will then **jab the ball upwards**, and either think about going for a **double touch**, or continue forward looking for a **demo**, followed by a **boost grab**.

After that, the 2nd man becomes the new **1st man** and can repeat the **jab cycle** until a high-percentage finish opens up.

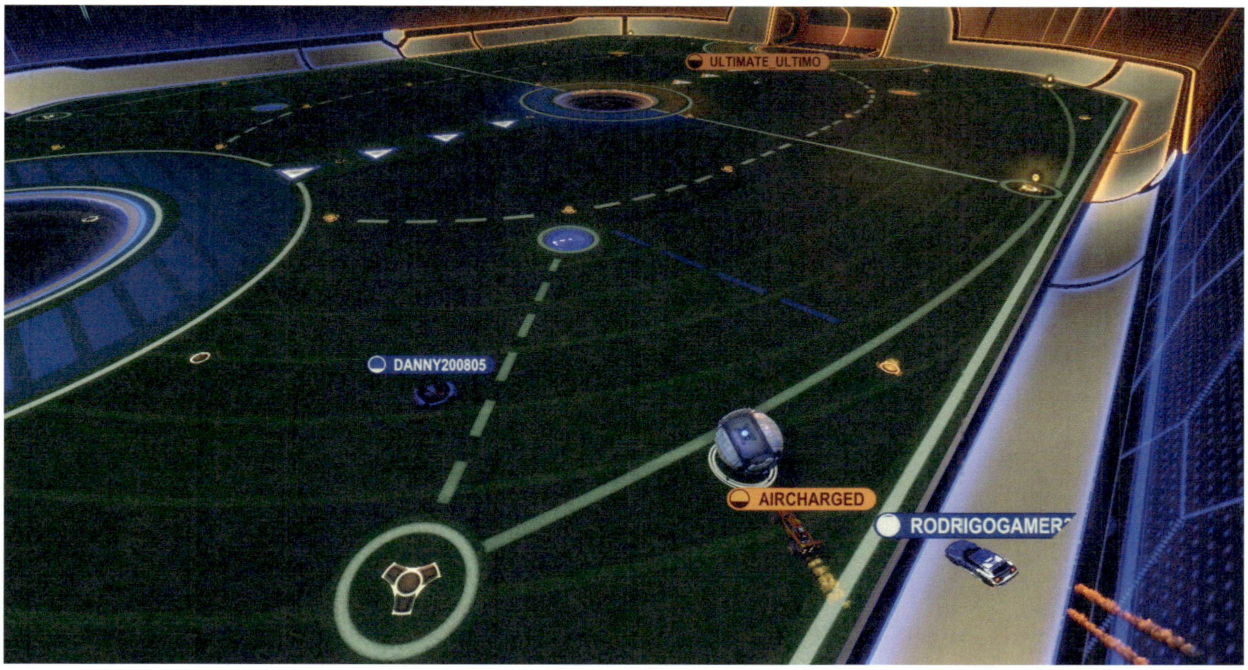

Pacifist Pivot 1: Dragging the ball out of the opponent's corner.

A tip with the Pacifist Pivot: It can be awkward to land if you are approaching the opponent's corner **head-on**, as reversing momentum in that spot often causes **bounces**.

To make it smoother, you can pivot **after** playing the ball across the **face of the opponent's net**, using the natural momentum coming **back towards your side**. This allows you to either make the **pivot pass** cleanly, or drag the ball back and begin setting up a **counterattack**.

Pacifist Pivot 2: Second man begins the jab cycle.

Kick-offs

There are many different kick-off techniques in Rocket League, Spanish kick-offs, fakes, delays, and more. If this were a general Rocket League guide, we would explore all of them. But in **The Pacifist System**, we keep things simple and reliable by using one primary approach, **the Dead Ball Kick-off**.

The aim of this kick-off is not necessarily to win the ball, but to **control** it. Our number one priority is to prevent the ball from going over us. To do this, we make our final jump for the ball slightly earlier than usual, ensuring that we contact the centre of the ball in height with the centre of our hitbox. This subtle adjustment reduces the upward lift on the ball. So, even if we lose the challenge, we lose it across the ground, not into the air, making recovery much easier.

Another **key benefit** of this kick-off style is that the ball often stays nearby. This allows our second man (the follower) to stay close and **immediately pressure the ball**. Ideally, the follower moves towards Pad 1 as the kick-off taker hits the ball, staying just close enough to react. The follower's job is to **apply fast pressure, grab boost if possible**, and **put the ball on net early**.

Notice how F_U_Z_E is on pad 1 as I hit the ball, this way he will be first to the ball in a safe manner. Any closer could be dangerous, and any further could lead to easy beats.

Do not shy away from taking a 50/50 here, kick-offs are chaotic, and there will not always be time to position perfectly.

If the ball spills out towards the mid boost, the second man should be the one to collect it. This gives them the opportunity to **launch a strong**, **immediate attack**, especially since the opposing team will likely be **disorganised** or **scrambling for boost**.

The beauty of this **early-jump technique** is that when it does win, **it really wins**. By striking from a higher point, your car can force the **ball over the opponent,** creating a **direct path to goal** and **quick scoring chances**.

Notice my contact point with the ball. It is higher than the opponents, and my car is flat, whereas the opponent has slight forward lean. This will be a successful kickoff for our team.

The Overall Strategy

Now that you have seen the system broken down piece by piece, let's bring it all together into a simple, actionable package.

When the opponents have possession, we **do not challenge head-on**. Instead, we **funnel them into our corner**, where their options are limited. Once they are committed, we either:

- **Take the ball across the net** and transition into offence.
- **Hold possession in the corner,** absorbing 50s until they overextend.

When they do overcommit, our **2nd man immediately takes over**, launching the counterattack. This is where we apply smart pressure, aiming shots, stealing big boosts, and hunting for demos.

Meanwhile, the **1st man (now rotating behind)** does not just collect random pads, they go straight to pad 1 or 2, or, as their awareness improves, they read the **loose ball** to either finish the play or jab it high to keep the attack alive.

This loop :

1. Contain.
2. Dispossess.
3. Counterattack.
4. Recycle.

Is the heartbeat of **The Pacifist System.**

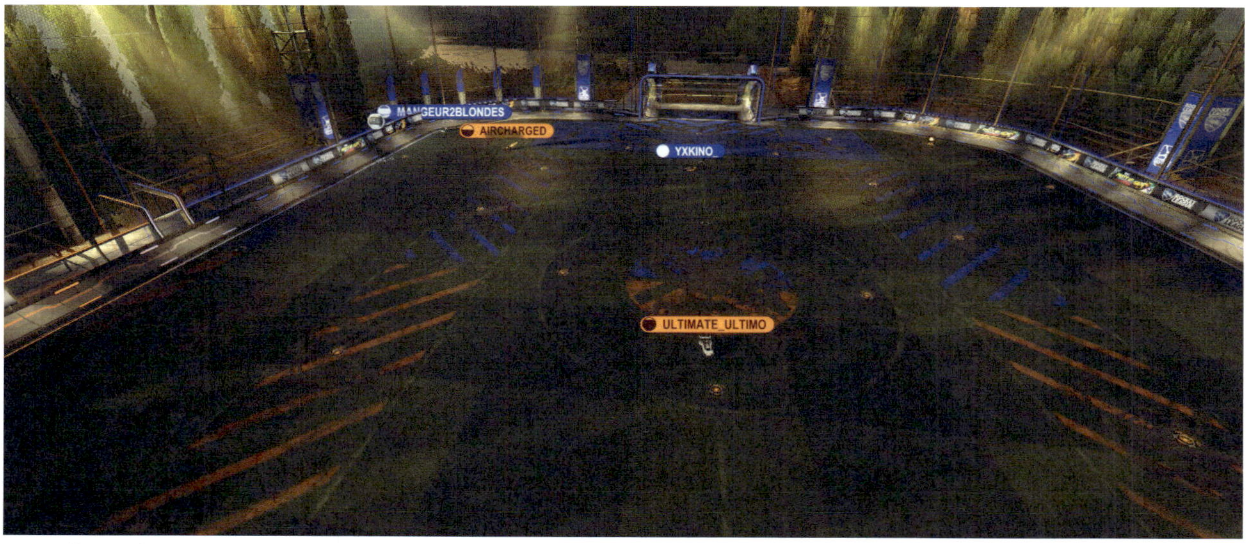

Full 1: They own the ball, so 1st man shadows inside, whilst 2nd man pads down the middle.

Full 2: The ball is successfully in the corner and 2nd man is in deep net facing out.

Full 3: The opponents overcommit allows 2nd man to get a free ball for the 2v1 counterattack.

Full 4: A successful counter that leads to a goal from the 2v1.

Conclusion

So that is **The Pacifist System**. A smarter, safer, more efficient way to play Rocket League built on pressure, control, and high-percentage decision-making.

You now understand how to defend with structure, create attacks with intention, and rotate in a way that protects your teammate while maximising opportunities. Whether you are the 1st man pressing in the corner, or the 2nd man sitting deep and waiting to strike, you have a clear job, and the tools to do it.

The biggest takeaway? This system removes guesswork. Instead of just diving into plays or hoping for mechanics to bail you out, you are now equipped to force bad decisions out of your opponents and then punish them for it.

If you have made it this far, you are already way ahead of most players.

But reading is not where it ends, this system is designed to be lived and trained, and that is why we have built the community around it.

If you want support, feedback, coaching, scrims, or just other players learning the same system, come join us in **The Pacifist System Discord** by using the QR code below. That is where everything happens. You will find coaching options, community drills, live sessions, replay reviews, and even a full free progression system where players level up their mechanics using the same structure that I have used to coach hundreds of players to new peak ranks.

And if you are ready to fully commit, you can book in for **1-on-1 coaching** or join the **next live cohort of The Pacifist System**, where we train together across six weeks with live calls, video breakdowns, and scrims, even against pros.

This book has given you the map. The Blueprint section is the next step where you will find complete **training plans and routines tailored to your current rank**. These will guide you through the drills and decisions you should focus on each week depending on where you are in your Rocket League journey. Whether you are aiming to break out of Gold, push into Champ, or lock in that first Grand Champ season title, these Blueprints will show you how.

Let's get to work.

BLUEPRINTS - ACHIEVE YOUR GOALS

There are countless ways to rank up, but these Blueprints are different. They are not just about doing drills or routines, they are about **thinking like a Pacifist player** and mastering core concepts at your current rank.

Each Blueprint gives you a 7-day training outline (with 2 rest days) focused on:

- Tactical mindset shift
- Mechanical focus
- Positional or decision-making upgrade

These sessions are short (20–30 minutes max), and may include a handful of targeted drills from the book. But the key is **intentional repetition**, paired with small ranked sessions (2–3 games only) played with focus.

Why? Because **endless grinding builds bad habits**. As you get tired, you will naturally go into autopilot. The more you do something, the more it sticks, so we need to make sure we are re-writing bad habits. Smart, focused practice builds Grand Champions.

Remember: These are not the only routines that work. But they are distilled from everything inside The Pacifist System, and they are designed to change how you see the game forever.

Bronze - Gold

Purpose: Build core foundations of the Pacifist System. Learn how to stop diving, maintain calm positioning, and start recognising when you are in danger, or when your opponent is.

Day	Drill 1	Notes	Drill 2	Notes
Monday *Mindset & Calm Defence*	Solo Funnel Drill 1F (2 matches)	Block the middle, get used to driving towards the screen. Your controls will be opposite, take your time, loses do not matter.	Counterattack Two Man Drill 8A (2 matches)	Recognise when you are in DD and use deep net accordingly as 2nd man. Do not push out of net, stay deep and wait for your turn.
Tuesday *Understanding Not To Challenge*	Solo Funnel Drill 1F (2 matches)	Same as yesterday, know that just positioning and being a blocker is effective to prevent the opponents from scoring.	Jab Drill 16A (10 minutes)	Focus not on power sliding, but instead go ahead of the ball and slow down to perform a tight turn, then boost and hit the ball.
Thursday *Second Man Mastery*	Counterattack Two Man Drill 8A (2 matches)	As before, when sat in deep net try and find the opponents 2nd man to guide your counterattack options.	Hybrid Shadow Drill 11A (10 minutes)	When attacking the net, tell your partner just to use ground balls for now. Slow down and get in the way of the net.
Friday *Backboard Awareness*	Corner Control Drill 3A (10 minutes)	Get used to controlling the ball toward the corner and then going up the backboard to block any high attacks.	Lockdown Backboard pack 20C1-273B-99B9-B96C	Follow the video if required, but essentially go ahead of the ball and whilst facing away, backflip / single jump so the ball hits you.
Saturday *Intro A Controlled Attack*	Basic Lateral Dribble Drill 13A (10 mins)	Focus on slowly controlling the ball from wing to wing. Try to ramp the speed slowly to prevent bounces.	Jab Plus Drill 16A (10 minutes)	Doing the jab drill, this time do a softer jab so the ball bounces up in front but still near your car, then drive underneath and jump to pop the ball up.

Gold - Platinum

Purpose: Strengthen control under pressure. Learn to reset before acting, slow the tempo, and develop awareness of second man positioning and safe shadowing.

Day	Drill 1	Notes	Drill 2	Notes
Monday *Shadow Reaction*	Perfect Side Flip Drill 1C (10 minutes)	Get close, and ensure the ball goes up the wall (does not bounce) when you do the side flip. Hit the middle of the ball to achieve.	Pincer Drill 2A (10 minutes)	Focus on reducing the amount of pincers you need to get close to the ball. Make sure you do NOT turn into your side flip.
Tuesday *Shadow Confidence*	Solo Funnel Drill 1F (2 matches)	Use the skills developed from yesterday to start adding in your perfect side flip.	Front End Perfect Side Flip Drill 1D (10 minutes)	Focus on developing your front-end aggression and not diving in, close the distance fast, then go into an inside shadow.
Thursday *Application Day*	1v1 ranked matches (2 matches)	Deliberately play slowly. Only challenge once you have performed a pincer. Observe if your calmness frustrates opponents.	Freeplay routine controlled play (10 minutes)	Use slow carries, bounce dribbles, and shadow path recreations. Boost should stay under 20 for most of the session.
Friday *Defensive Defence*	Counterattack Two Man Drill 8A (10 minutes)	Work on seeing everything. This is your default position in solo queue when collapsed. Try and make your counters count.	2nd Man Shadow Drill 9A (10 minutes)	Focus on staying with the ball after you side flip it to the corner.
Saturday *2nd Man Offensive Defence*	Trigger Drill 10A (10 mins)	Focus on spotting when the ball has gone passed the trigger, and instantly fall into net.	Hybrid Shadow Drill 11A (10 minutes)	Try and alternate between being early and clearing the ball outwards. And being late and defending the ball towrads the backboard or corner.

Platinum - Diamond

Purpose: Refine tempo and transition play. Learn how to control bounce dribbles, punish second man mistakes, and stop throwing away counterattacks.

Day	Drill 1	Notes	Drill 2	Notes
Monday *Bounce Control & Jab Timing*	Power Shot (Rising) Drill 17B (10 minutes)	Practice letting the ball lightly touch the side of your car on the way up. Use minimal boost. Power shot just before the opponents third on the upward bounce.	Jab Drill 16A (10 minutes)	Focus on a smooth power slide around the ball. Do a medium jab with a slight angle, so you can transition to a bounce dribble power shot.
Tuesday *Punish Overcommit*	Trigger Drill 10A (10 minutes)	Once the trigger has been pressed. Go into opposite side deep net and then complete the counterattack as fast as possible.	Counterattack Two Man Drill 8A (10 minutes)	Once you start the counterattack ensure a finish, ideally via a power shot.
Thursday *Application Day*	2v2 ranked matches (2 matches)	Use the goal of baiting the opponent to the corner to punish them. No panic plays. Score from mistakes, not chaos.	Freeplay routine bounce dribble focus (10 minutes)	Control the bounce, set up flicks, let the ball fall and then hit it. Avoid jumping unless there is a clear reason.
Friday *Offensive Defence*	Solo Funnel Drill Drill 1F (2 matches)	Work on getting much closer to the player before they can begin. Instant side flips or single jumps to frustrate them.	2nd Man Shadow Drill 9A (10 minutes)	Focus on staying with the ball after you side flip it to the corner. Then instantly tap the ball off the wall and finish with a bounce dribble power shot.
Saturday *Pressure Conversion*	2v2 ranked matches (2 matches)	Ensure you are shadowing to the corners. Once on offence, use multiple jabs into demos / big boost grabs to keep the opponents pinned.	Pacifist Pivot Wrap Drill 19A (10 minutes)	Try and keep the jab sequence going as long as possible. See if as a duo you can beat 5 jabs to the backboard.

Diamond - Champ

Purpose: Break into high-level decision-making. Learn to manipulate defenders with jab tempo, react to overcommits, and punish with speed or delay based on threat level.

Day	Drill 1	Notes	Drill 2	Notes
Monday *Transition Recognition*	In Game Counterattack Two Man Drill 8A (2 matches)	In ranked 2v2, work on purposely using the counterattack how you have been practicing.	In Game Pacifist Pivot Wrap Drill 19A (2 matches)	In a real ranked game, try and purposely score from a pacifist pivot. Remember the easiest way it to go across the opponents net and then out into the 2nd man.
Tuesday *Offensive Offence*	Power Slide Cut Drill 14C (10 minutes)	Spend 5 minutes going for power slide cut outplays. Then spend 5 minutes using the cut to set up a carry and finish with a flick.	Instant Flick Drill 15A (10 minutes)	Work on getting as much height as possible on these flicks to completely blind opponents. I have hit the ceiling in the past!
Thursday *Application Day*	2v2 ranked matches (2 matches)	Start each play with a jab, or, if the ball is already up, single jump into it to keep it high. The goal is to hit the ball over the opponents. Use a slight angle to avoid dunks.	Freeplay routine bounce dribble and delays (10 minutes)	Practise bounce control into short flicks or stop-fakes. Force yourself to pause mid-possession and scan.
Friday *Pressure Review*	Replay review (10-15 minutes)	Look at how often your own challenges lead to counter attacks. Focus on avoidable touches and poor second man timing.	Bounce dribble review (10 minutes)	Record yourself doing bounce dribbles. Watch it back, are you wasting boost, are you using too many inputs? Make the movement smooth!
Saturday *Movement Control*	Corner Control Drill 3A (10 minutes)	Start to use dodges or single jumps into the ball to drag the ball back at greater speeds.	Snaking Drill 5A (10 minutes)	Try and keep your boost levels high by only tapping it when turning in.

Champ - Grand Champ

Purpose: Finalise your decision-making mastery. Learn to delay without stalling, challenge with intent, and apply The Pacifist System with speed and calm under Grand Champ pressure.

Day	Drill 1	Notes	Drill 2	Notes
Monday *Brick Wall*	Lateral Dribble 50s Drill 13B-D (15 minutes)	You can either do each drill for 5 minutes, or focus on one specific drill each week. The goal is to choose the right 50 based on the opponent.	Replay review (1 match)	Focus on every single 50/50 you lost. Were you side on to the ball? Were you positioned inside? Was it unwinnable, and therefore turning away would be smart?
Tuesday *Hook To Finish*	Hook Shot Drill 14A (10 minutes)	Try and get the energy into the ball so that it absolutely flies at the net. 110kph is the goal here.	Freeplay hook shot focus (10 minutes)	In freeplay work on using hook shots off the walls and then shooting them directly towards the net.
Thursday *Timing The Challenge*	In game snaking to challenge (2 matches)	Now you should be proficient at snaking. Try and time a real challenge. Do this in 1v1. Time the challenge for when the opponent jabs the ball forward.	Defending From Behind Drill 1E (10 minutes)	Work on instantly chasing the opponent down and hiting the ball into your corner as you go back to defence.
Friday *Hover*	Hover For Ground Air Dribble Drill 7A (10 minutes)	Focus on getting up early and then maintaining boost to stay high.	Hover For Wall Air Dribble Drill 7B (10 minutes)	Try not to be too wide here, think about the line of the attack.
Saturday *Certification Day*	Self-coached 2v2 (2 matches)	Go in with the knowledge you have from the book. Can you spot your mistakes live? Can you preempt dives and punish structure breaks?	Freeplay flow (10 minutes)	No thinking, just play with the rules deep in your muscle memory. Let the system express itself.

THE DRILLS

This section contains all of the **core drills** used within **The Pacifist System** main cohort. These drills represent the foundation of the system and are designed to build the key mechanics, habits, and decision-making patterns needed to climb through the ranks, from Gold to Grand Champion and beyond.

Many drills also have variations that are explored in coaching sessions or custom sessions within the Discord community. If a drill resonates with you or targets a clear weakness in your game, do not be afraid to repeat it or adapt it into your own routine.

Drill 1A - Funnel To Corner

- **Setup**: Player A starts with the ball in the corner.
- Player B begins on the **inside of the ball**, blocking the centre of the field.
- Player A then dribbles toward the opposite corner, allowing Player B to **guide them using inside shadowing.**
- Once at the far corner, **swap roles and repeat** the drill heading back.
- **Keep the ball grounded** for now to simplify.
- Recommended as a **warm-up drill for Champ 1 and below**, 5 minutes daily for at least a week.

Drill 1B - Front-end To Funnel

- **Setup**: Player A starts with the ball in the corner.
- Player B begins on **boost pad 1** (the pad before halfway line, centre of the field).
- Player B **flips toward the inside** (not directly at the ball), then **power slide and turn away** from the ball.
- When Player B **taps boost**, Player A begins the dribble.
- The drill plays out the same as Drill 1A, now with added approach practice

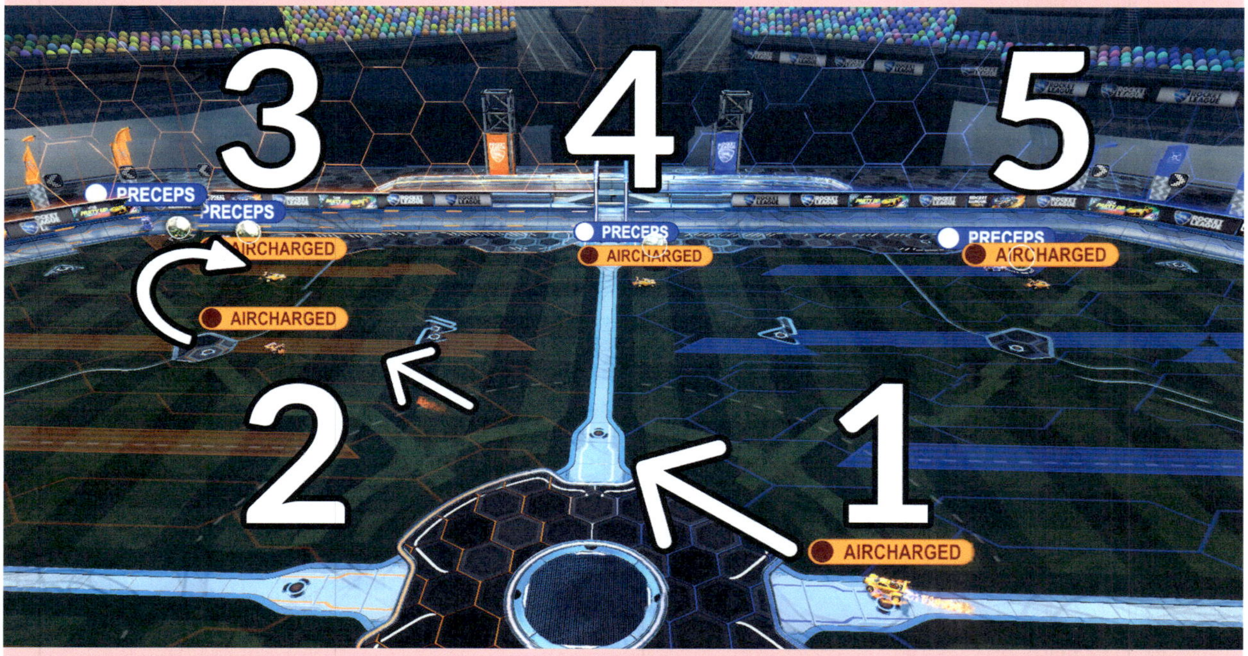

Drill 1C - Perfect Side Flip

- **Setup**: Same as Drill 1A.
- Player B is near Player A in the corner.
- As soon as Player A pushes the ball down the wing, Player B tries to **successfully land a perfect side flip challenge**.
- The goal is for the ball to **roll up and away** from Player A into the corner.
- Both players stay near the ball, repeating **multiple side flips** until they reach the corner. Then switch.

Drill 1D - Front End Perfect Side Flip

- **Setup**: Same as Drill 1B.
- Player B starts on boost pad 1, Player A in the corner.
- Player B flips toward Player A, who pushes the ball down the wing.
- Player B attempts to **perfect side flip challenge** the ball as soon as possible, sending it into the corner.
- Repeat side flips until corner is reached, then swap roles.

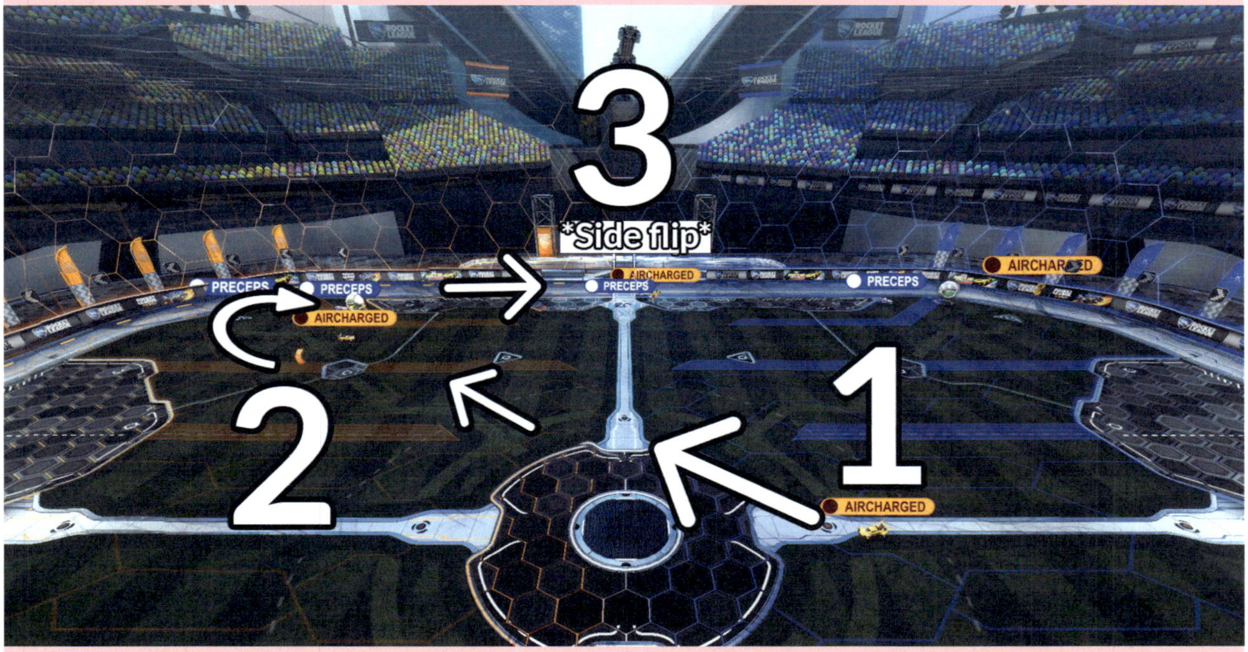

Drill 1E - Defending From Behind

- **Setup**: Player A starts in the corner with the ball
- Player B starts in Player A's net.
- As Player A begins to **slowly move the ball forward**, Player B **boosts / flips** out of net towards Player A.
- Once Player B is close enough, they will either **bump / demo** Player A, or, jump over them and hit the ball to their corner.
- Repeat using various dribbles, such as a carry.

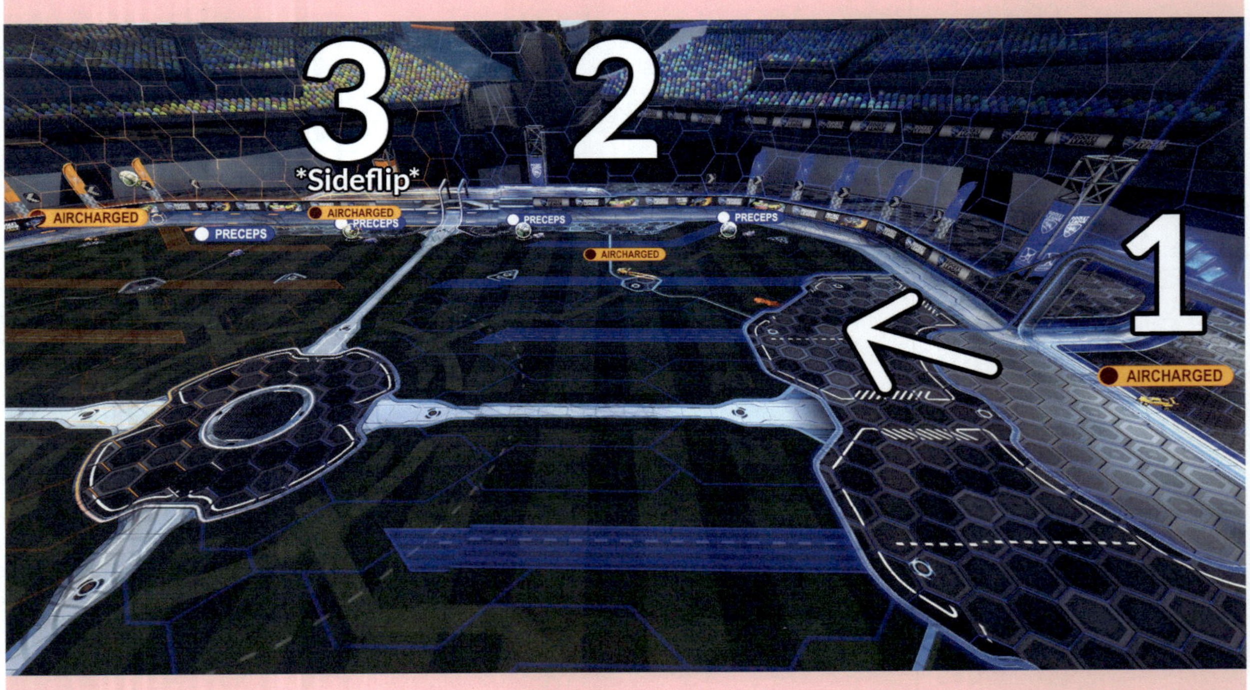

Drill 1F - Solo Funnel

- **Setup**: Head into **casual 1v1 match** (ideally Vs. players slightly lower ranked).
- **Focus on practice, not winning.**
- Allow your opponent to take possession, then:
    - Shadow from an inside position.
    - Try to force them toward the corner.
    - Use perfect side flips to block or deflect awkward plays.

Drill 2A - Pincer

- **Setup**: Player A starts with the ball in the corner.
- Player B starts on **boost pad 2** (the pad just after the halfway line) facing the same side that Player A is on.
- **Player A** pushes the ball forward along the wing.
- **Player B** uses **front-end aggression** to close the space with **mini pincer movements.**
- **Once close enough**, Player B performs a perfect side flip challenge.
- **Repeat** the drill by swapping roles.

Drill 3A - Corner Control

- **Setup**: Solo drill in Free Play. Start with the ball rolling into your own corner.
- Let the ball rise up the wall, then **drive up the wall ahead of it**, positioning your car **slightly above** the ball and between it and the centre of your goal.
- Stay in this position as the ball climbs, using **braking** to maintain a safe buffer zone with the ball acting as a shield, making it hard for any would-be challenger to demo you.
- Once the ball peaks and begins to fall, **stay on the wall and come down with it**, keeping an **inside position**. The goal is to **caress the ball** gently with the **side of your car**, maintaining control without overcommitting. If the opponent were to stay close, you would remain above the ball on the backboard.
- As the ball lands, aim to keep possession or transition into a controlled clear or pass.

Drill 3B - Corner Half Flip

- **Setup**: Solo drill in Free Play. Start with the ball rolling into your own corner.
- Let the ball rise up the wall, then **drive up ahead of it**, taking an **inside position** and **matching the height** of the ball on the wall or backboard.
- As the ball peaks and begins to fall, remain above or level with it, acting as a shield from any imaginary demo or pressure below.
- This time, instead of staying with the ball, **use a half-flip** (or backflip if you prefer) to gently knock the ball **back toward the corner**.
- The goal is to **softly reset the play**, avoiding pressure while staying close enough to re-engage with the next touch or support your teammate.
- This drill can be done with various timings on the half-flip to keep the opponents guessing.

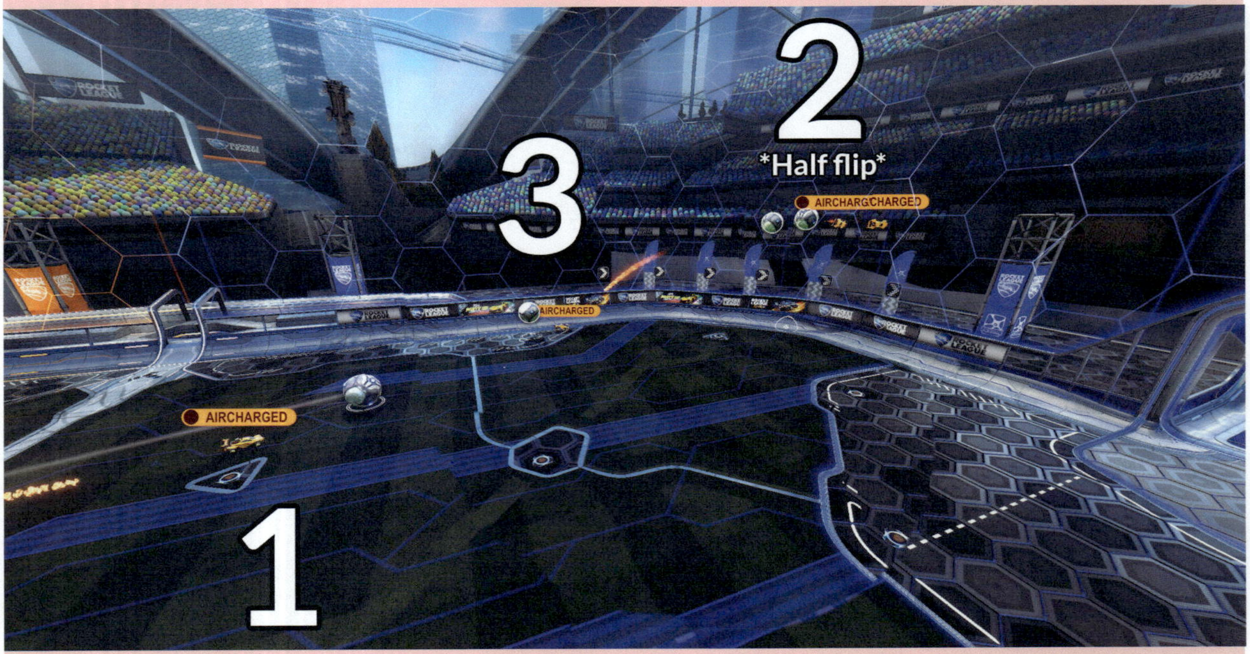

Drill 3C - Corner Half Flip Two Man Version

- **Setup**: Two-player drill. Player A starts with the ball rolling into their own corner. Player B begins just behind or slightly outside the play, ready to pressure.
- Player A lets the ball roll up the wall and **drives up ahead of it**, taking an **inside position** and **matching the height** of the ball on the wall or backboard.
- Player B immediately begins driving up the wall, aiming to **demo Player A**.
- Player A's job is to use the ball as a **shield**, staying between the ball and their opponent to **block the demo** attempt.
- As the ball peaks and starts to drop, **Player A either stays with the ball, half-flips or backflips** to knock the ball **safely back toward the corner** while avoiding the demo and **staying close** for the next play.
- Rotate roles after each attempt, focusing on **timing, positioning**, and **calm** recovery under demo pressure.

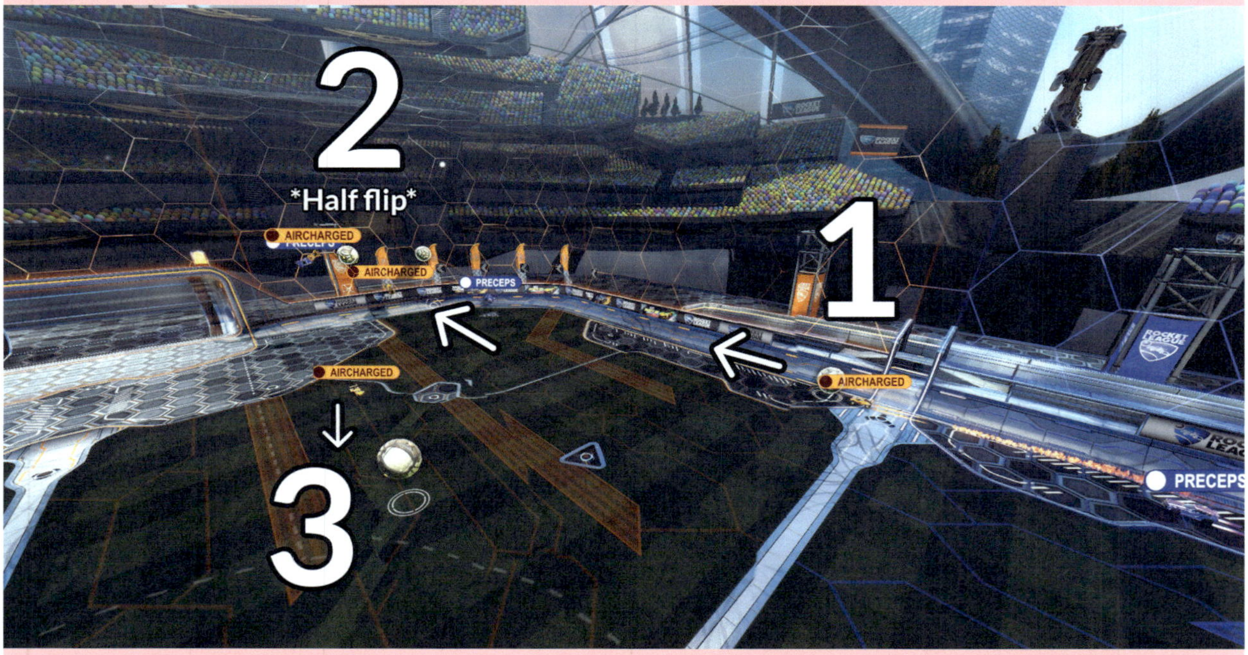

Drill 4A - Triangle Defending

- **Setup:** Player A starts with the ball in the corner.
- Player B starts nearby.
- Player A takes the ball across their net towards the opposite corner boost.
- Player B goes ahead of Player A once they know what they are trying to do and **steals the corner boost.**
- Player B then heads towards the mid boost, allowing Player A to attack the middle.
- **With the boost advantage, Player B challenges Player A with a perfect side flip.**
- If done correctly, the ball should barrel over Player A, creating a scoring opportunity for Player B.

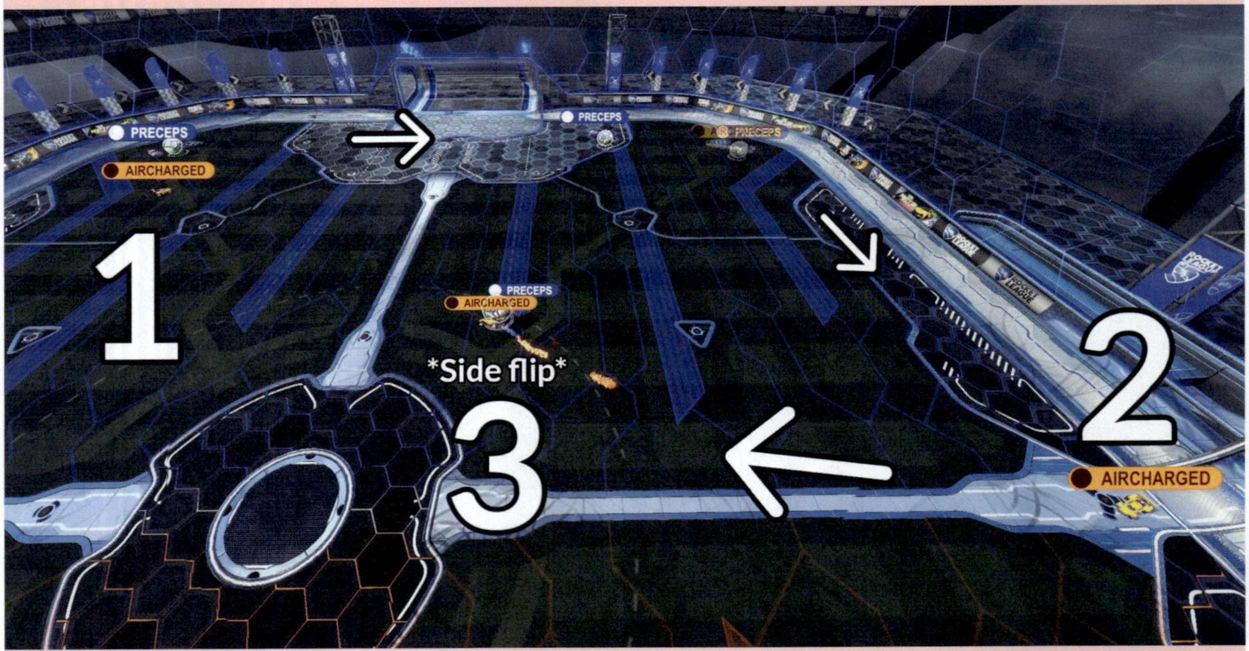

Drill 4B - Triangle Defending From Save

- **Setup:** Player A starts in net. Player B begins near the midfield line with the ball in front of them.
- Player B shoots a saveable shot at Player A who saves it to the corner.
- Player B immediately reads the direction of the save and **collects the corner boost.**
- Player A remains on the ball, now with low or no boost.
- Knowing they hold a boost advantage, Player B drives to mid-boost and allows Player A to stay on the play.
- Player B staying wide allows Player A to take the centre. As Player A pushes the ball toward mid, Player B collapses with a **perfect side flip** challenge.
- Swap roles after each round.

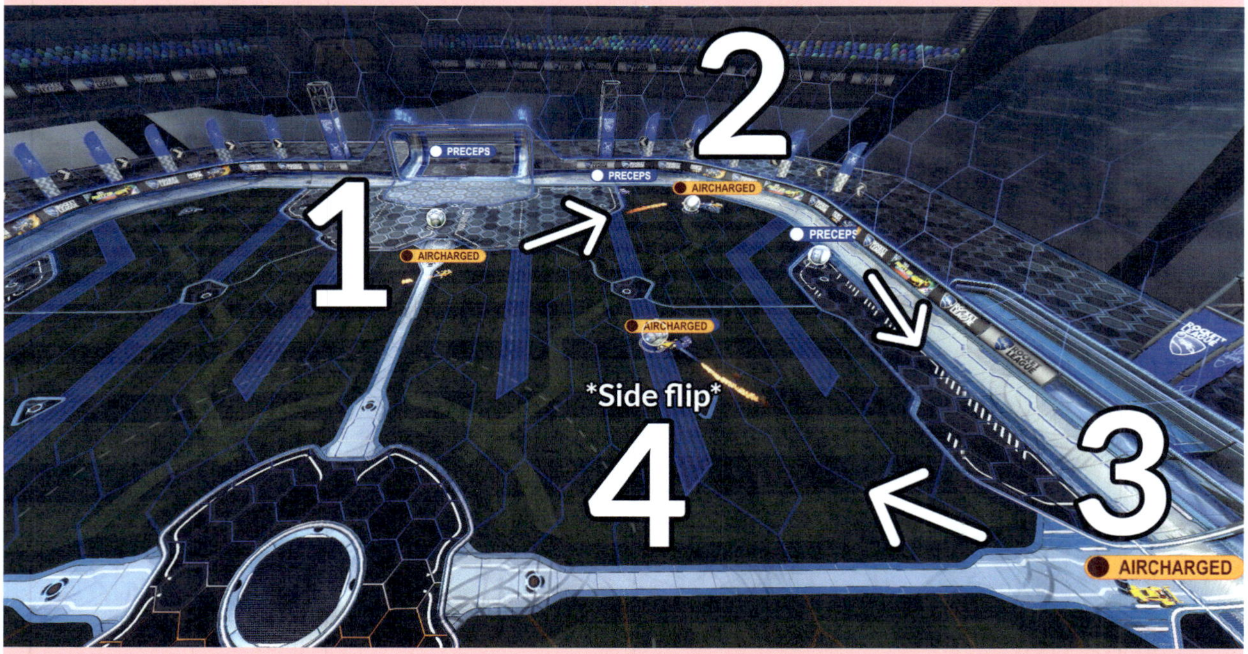

Drill 5A - Snaking

- **Setup:** Player A starts with the ball in their own corner.
- Player B approaches with front-end aggression and enters an inside shadow position.
- Player B stays slightly further back than usual, assuming Player A has control.
- Player B then begins snaking, using a figure-8 movement to pop in and out of view from inside and outside shadow positions.
- The goal is to **force a mistake or panic touch** from Player A without overcommitting.

Drill 5A - Snaking With Challenge

- **Setup:** Player A starts with the ball in their own corner.
- Player B approaches with front-end aggression and enters an inside shadow position.
- Player B stays slightly further back than usual, assuming Player A has control.
- Player B then begins snaking, using a **figure-8 movement** to pop in and out of view from **inside** and **outside** shadow positions.
- At any point during the movement, Player B may choose to challenge the ball when hidden behind it.
- This teaches both pressure timing and the ability to read hesitation in the opponent's play.

Drill 6A - Team Drag Back

- **Setup:** This is a **team drill**. **Player A** starts on their corner boost, **Player B** has the ball and starts on **mid boost same side.**
- **Player B** begins to **push the ball toward their own corner**.
- **Player A** chases and stays grounded in the corner to create realistic pressure.
- **As the ball approaches the corner, Player B should peel off** and move **inside** the ball's path, then head **up the backboard**.
- **Player B should now be slightly inside and above the ball.**
  - If the ball has **low momentum**, stay above it, let it drop, and **take control on the ground**. Play it to the **opposite corner** and continue the drill.
  - If the ball is going **high**, let it **graze the side of your car** on the backboard to **kill the bounce**, then take control and push to the opposite corner.

Drill 7A - Hover For Ground Air Dribble

- **Setup:** Player A starts in the middle of the pitch. Player B begins in their own net.
- Player B pushes the ball toward Player A, then quickly turns around and gets into a shadow position.
- Player A jabs the ball and begins an **air dribble** toward the net.
- Player B gets in the **shadow position**, then jumps up early to **hover and block** the air dribble.
- Repeat, switching roles after several attempts.

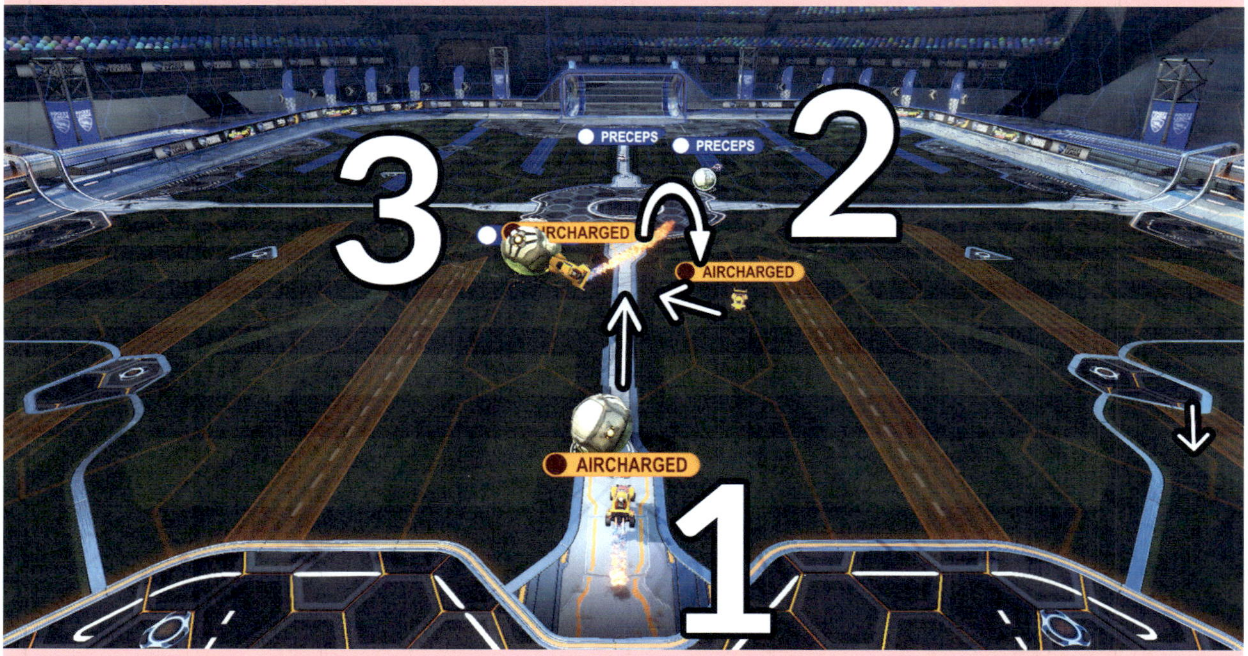

Drill 7B - Hover For Wall Air Dribble

- **Setup:** Player A starts at the ball spawn location with the ball. Player B waits nearby.
- As Player A pushes the ball toward the wall, Player B moves near the ball and then peels away as it begins to roll up the wall.
- Player A begins an **air dribble** from the wall.
- Player B immediately **double jumps and flies up** to hover and match the ball's height.
- If you are new to this, start with **outside shadowing** to avoid own goals. Switch to **inside shadowing** as aerial control improves.
- Focus on **matching the ball's height** and forcing Player A into an awkward touch.
- Repeat the drill several times, switching roles when ready.

Drill 7C - Hover For Wall Air Dribble Full Map

- **Setup:** Player A starts in their back corner with the ball. Player B is nearby.
- Player A pushes the ball across to the opposite back corner and begins a **wall air dribble**.
- Player B realising they cannot catch Player A, then backs off to **mid boost**.
- As Player A takes off, Player B **jumps and hovers**, trying to match the ball's height.
- Try to **challenge from below** if they are going high, or **from above** if they stay low.
- Aim to **stop the ball or guide it to the corner** to regain possession.
- Swap roles after several attempts.

Drill 8A - Counterattack Two Man

- **Setup: Player A** starts in their **corner** with the ball. **Player B** is on the **same team**, positioned **deep in net**.
- **Player A** hits the ball **around the corner** to set up **Player B**.
- **As soon as Player A** hits the ball, they will **back off** to prepare for a potential **counterattack**.
- **Player B**, from the **deep net position**, takes a **shot on the opponent's net** and **immediately pushes up** for the **finish**.
- **If Player B** cannot finish, they should **maintain momentum** and pretend to **demo a defender**.
    - If the **demo opportunity** is not there, **do not overcommit** into the opponent's net.
    - Instead, **peel off** and collect the **corner boost**.

Drill 8B - Counterattack Three Man

- **Setup:** Player A starts in their corner with the ball. Player B is on the same team and in the net. Player C starts on the mid boost on the same side.
- Player C dives on the ball.
- Player A allows Player C to **hit the ball around the corner**.
- Player B, who is deep in net, **shoots the ball at the opponents' net** and instantly **pushes up for the finish**.
- Player C tries to rotate back and defend (but won't be able to), while **Player A follows the play as quickly** as possible to ensure **Player C ends up behind the play**.
- If Player B cannot finish, they should **maintain momentum**, **grab the corner boost**, and **leave the ball for Player A** to continue the attack.

Drill 8C - Counterattack Four Man

- **Setup:** Same as 8B but with Player D waiting directly in the middle of the pitch.
- Same drill as 8B, but this time Player D will **collapse and attempt a shadow save**, forcing them into the net.
- Player B will then either **look for a demo** or **grab the boost and the ball** as it goes to the corner. From there, **Player B will look for a Pacifist Pivot** to Player A to begin the jab attacks.
- Player C **tries to rotate back and defend** (but won't be able to), while Player A **follows the play quickly** to ensure Player C ends up behind the play.
- If Player B **cannot finish**, they should **maintain momentum, grab the corner boost**, and **leave the ball for Player A** to continue the attack.
- This drill can be performed with Player D in multiple different positions to test various counters.

Drill 9A - 2nd Man Shadow

- **Setup:** Solo drill In Free Play.
- **Reset the ball** at midfield.
- Get inline with the ball and begin driving back **towards your own net**, directly down the middle.
- **Press left on the D-pad** to trigger the ball to move towards your net.
- As the ball moves, **position yourself slightly inside** the path of the ball.
- From this inside angle, **side flip outwards**, staying **close to the ball** as you follow it.

Drill 10A - Trigger

- **Setup:** Player A has the ball in their corner.
- **Player B** (opposite team) starts near the ball in an **inside shadow** position.
- **Player C** (same team as Player B) is on **Pad 1** facing their own net.
- Player A begins pushing the ball. Player B **funnels** them into the corner.
- As they **pass the trigger pad**, Player C **swings into deep net** on the opposite side of the net.
- Player A then **overcommits** and shoots the ball into the corner.
- As soon as the ball is shot, Player A **retreats** to defend.
- Player B and C will then counterattack using **The Pacifist System**.

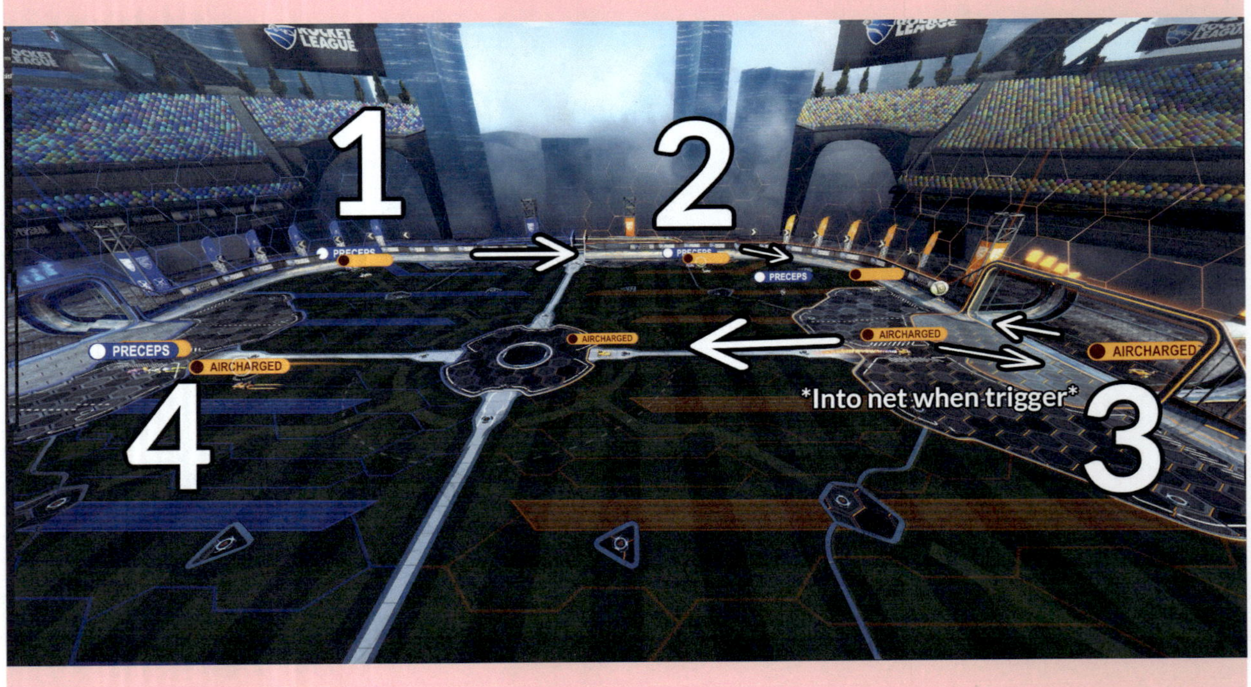

Drill 11A - Hybrid Shadow

- **Setup:** Player A has the ball in their half.
- **Player B** is on **Pad 1** facing their own net.
- **Player A** begins attacking via the wing, aiming to approach from a wide angle.
- **Player B** must avoid collapsing too deep, as they are the last man and have no support if beaten.
- **Player B** stays mostly central with a slight bias towards the side Player A is attacking from.
- As the attack develops, **Player B** must make a split-second decision:
    - **Early**: If they can make it into net before the shot, they may go for a traditional deep net save.
    - **Late:** If they are not early enough, they must stay forward and perform a **hybrid shadow save**, attempting to block the shot either before, during, or just after it hits the backboard.

Drill 12A - Common Situation

- **Setup:** Player A is attacking **Player B's corner**.
- **Player C** (Player B's teammate) is in **deep net**.
- **Player D** (Player A's teammate) is on **Pad 2**.
- Player A and Player B work to **intentionally create a 50/50** that spills the ball **centrally**.
- As the ball spills middle, **Player C rushes** out to challenge the shot, while **Player B retreats to the backboard** to defend potential aerials or double taps.
- **Player D** attempts to **outplay Player C**, either going over or around them.
- Meanwhile, **Player A attempts to bump or demo Player B** on the backboard.
- The **goal for the defending team** (Player B and C) is to **successfully nullify the attack** using strong positioning, awareness, and communication.

Drill 13A - Basic Lateral Dribble

- **Setup:** Solo drill in Free Play
- Start in your own corner with the ball. You can get the ball there by dribbling or by pressing **down on the D-pad** once positioned.
- Smoothly push the ball toward the **opponents opposite trigger pad**. Your focus is on gradually increasing speed without causing a bounce.
- Once the ball is rolling, move side-on behind it and try to **drive at a matching pace**, maintaining control and alignment. The goal is to stay side on to the ball the whole way.

Drill 13B - Single Jump 50/50 From Lateral

- **Setup:** Two-player drill. Player A starts with the ball in their own corner, as in Drill13A. Player B begins on the nearby **trigger boost** on the same side.
- Player A begins a **lateral dribble**, gently pushing the ball across the pitch while staying slightly behind and to the side of it.
- As the ball moves, Player A rotates into a **side-on position**, using their car to hide behind the ball and bait a challenge.
- Player B drives into the ball and **flips through** it to simulate a realistic 50/50. For now, they should **avoid supersonic speed**.
- As Player A sees the challenge coming, they perform a **single jump** at the last moment to win or absorb the 50/50 and land with possession.
- The goal is for Player A to **maintain control** and come away with **free space ahead** after the challenge.
- You can practice different variants such as having Player B **jab the ball.**

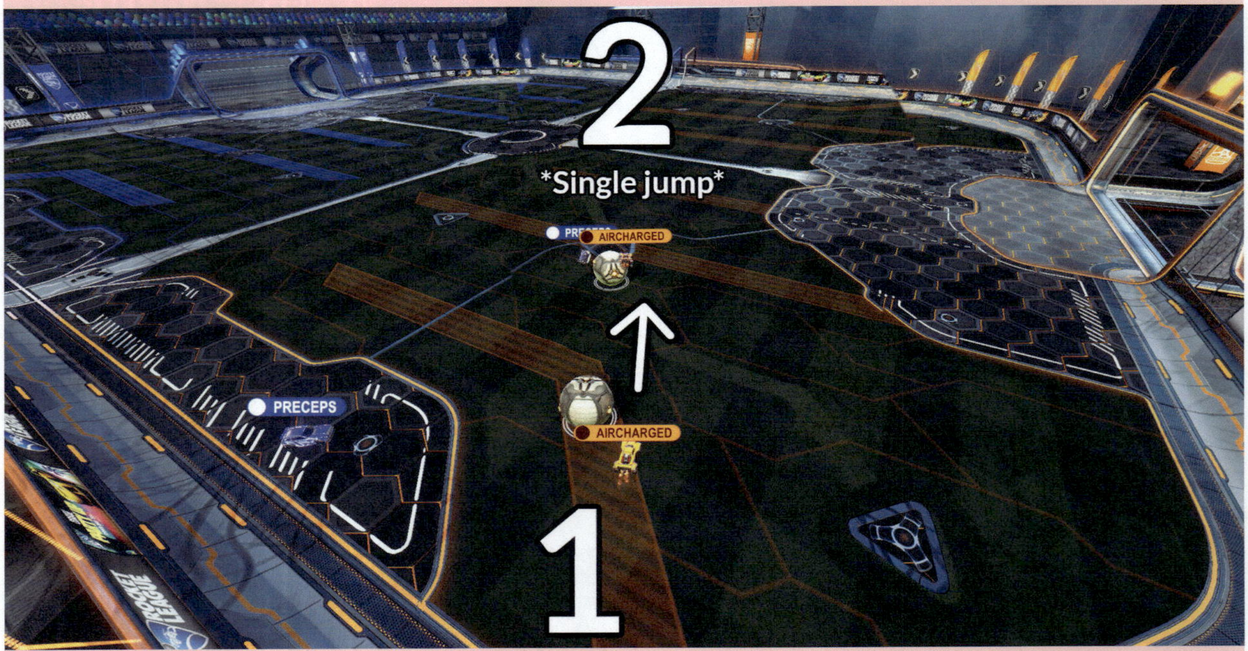

Drill 13C - Fadeaway 50/50 From Lateral

- **Setup:** Two-player drill. Player A starts with the ball in their own corner, as in Drill13A. Player B begins on the nearby **trigger boost** on the same side.
- Player A begins a **lateral dribble**, immediately getting behind the ball and preparing to **fadeaway**.
- Player B closes the gap quickly and **dives into the challenge**. This should be done with **minimal boost and low momentum**, as fadeaway situations typically happen in close quarters with limited resources.
- Player A absorbs the challenge by turning away and allowing Player B to **overcommit** into the ball.
- The goal is for Player A to **soak up the pressure** and come away with a free ball and time to counter.

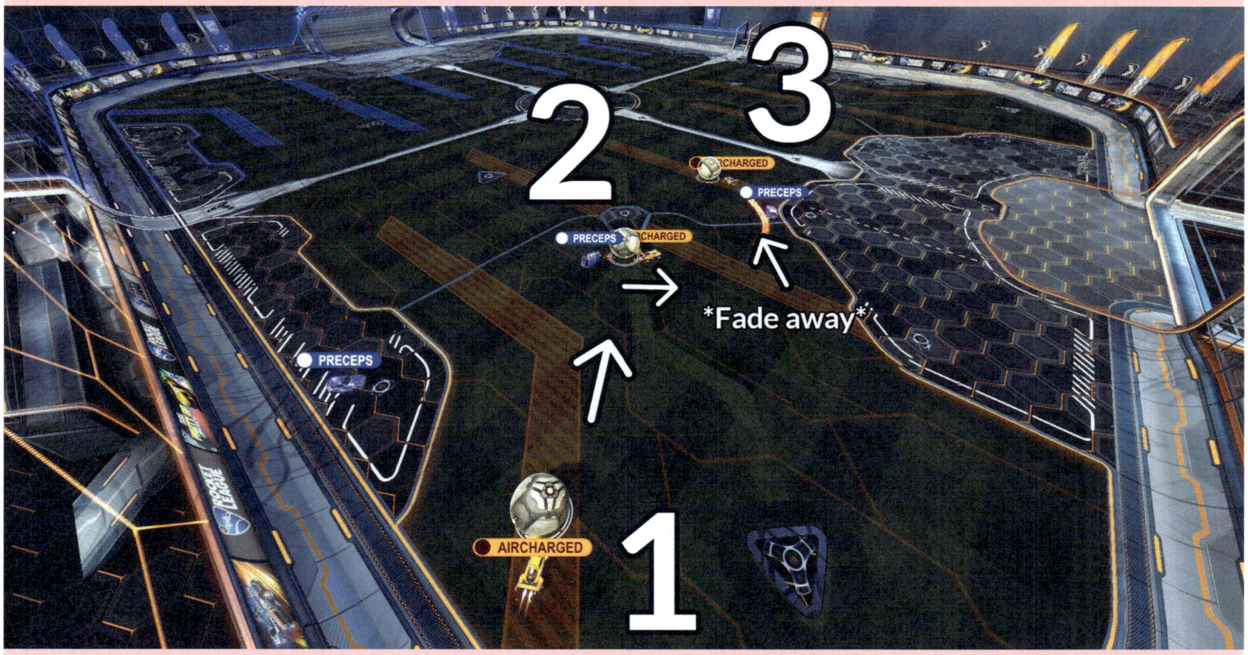

Drill 13D - Side Flip 50/50 From Lateral

- **Setup:** Two-player drill. Player A starts with the ball in their own corner, as in Drill13A. Player B begins on the **mid boost** on the same side.
- Player A begins a **lateral dribble**, ramping the ball speed smoothly and then rotating behind the ball as they spot Player B approaching.
- Player B closes the gap quickly and **dives into the challenge**, aiming to arrive at **supersonic speed.**
- Player A **jumps, when expecting the dive** and immediately performs a **side flip on impact**, using their car's larger side hitbox to avoid getting pushed back and to spill the ball into space behind Player B.
- The goal is for Player A to **win the 50/50** and end up with a **free ball** in open space.
- This drill can also be varied by having Player B throw in **jab-style mini challenges** to keep Player A honest.

Drill 14A - Hook Shot

- **Setup:** Solo drill in Free Play. Start with the ball in your own corner, exactly as in the earlier lateral-dribble drills.
- **Push the ball smoothly** toward the opponent's far-side **trigger pad**, keeping it flat and controlled.
- While **gradually increasing speed, dive away** to get slightly ahead of the ball.
- **Cut back in** with a tight hooking turn and meet the ball nose-first.
- Focus on striking **with your nose** to keep the contact consistent, aim to reach **supersonic** right at impact.
- Once the basic motion feels natural, vary your **contact points and timings** to place the shot into different parts of the goal.

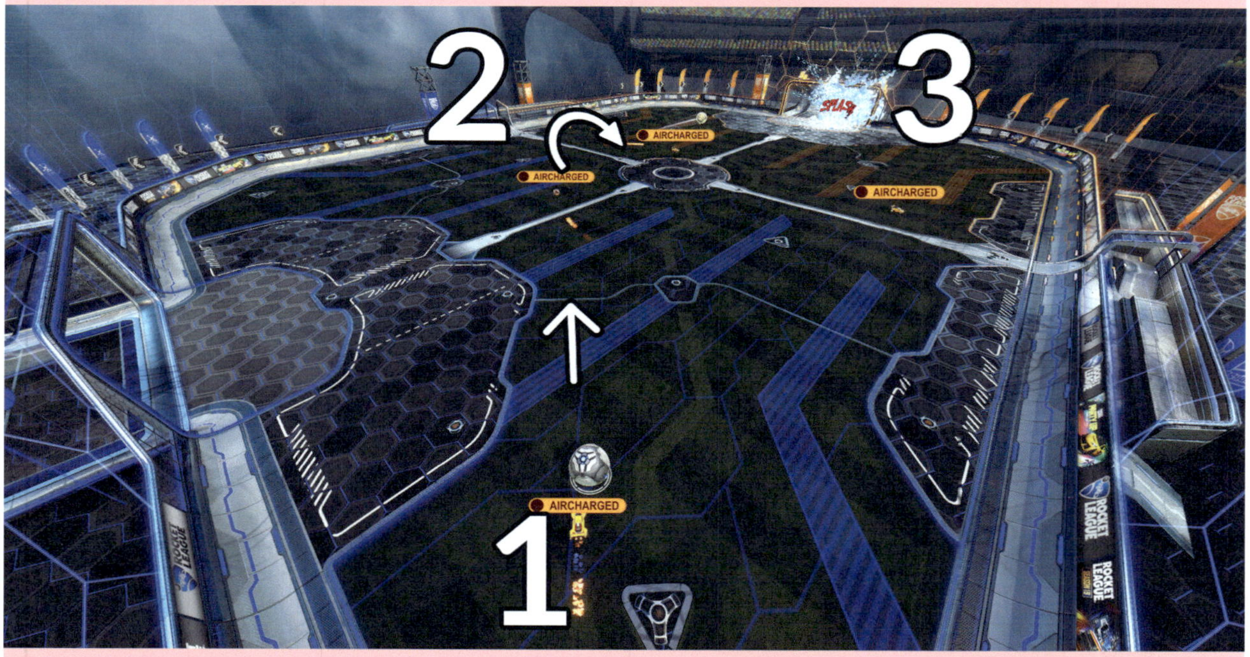

Drill 14B - Power Slide

- **Setup:** Solo drill in Free Play. Start on your half and choose a few **boost pads** or corners of the pitch as turning markers.
- Begin driving in **slow circles or figure-8s**, focusing on turning **without using boost**. Stay tight and controlled, **slow is key**.
- As the car turns, begin **feathering power slide** at the point where the turn naturally tightens. Adjust your **stick angle** to feel the car curving around the turn.
- Add occasional **brake taps** if you feel yourself drifting too wide, this helps tighten your path without spinning out.
- You can **boost into or out of turns** to recover even quicker once this is mastered.

Drill 14C - Power Slide Cut

- **Setup:** Solo drill in Free Play. Start with the ball in your own corner, exactly as in the earlier lateral-dribble drills.
- **Push the ball** out and begin dribbling laterally. Focus on matching the ball's speed and flow.
- **Switch lanes** and get slightly ahead of the ball, staying close and in control.
- As you begin to **pass the ball, slow down** slightly and then **power slide into a sharp cut**, turning back into the ball for a quick directional change.
- This drill builds control and confidence, **you are not trying to score**, just perfect the movement.
- In-game, this move should be used **early**, especially before reaching the **front post**, to avoid exposing the net and creating a scoring opportunity for your opponent.

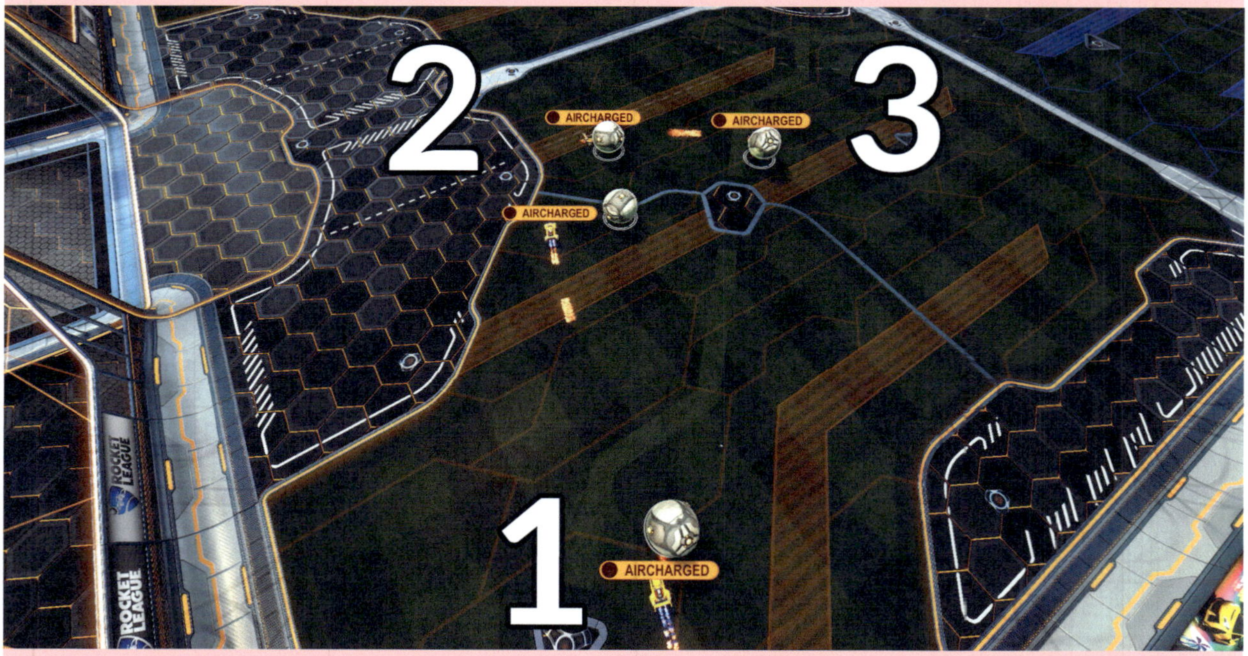

Drill 14D - Power Slide Cut Two Man

- **Setup:** Two-player drill. Player A starts in the corner with the ball. Player B begins on the **mid boost** on the same side.
- Player A begins **pushing the ball out** and starts a lateral dribble.
- As soon as the ball is in motion, **Player B dives** in for an instant challenge.
- Player A responds with an **immediate power slide cut**, executing the move **proactively** before Player B can get close.
- The aim is to simulate performing the move early, forcing a fast directional change to beat the challenge.
- In real games, if the opponent backs off, this same power slide can be used later to transition into a **bounce dribble, carry**, or even a **hook shot**.

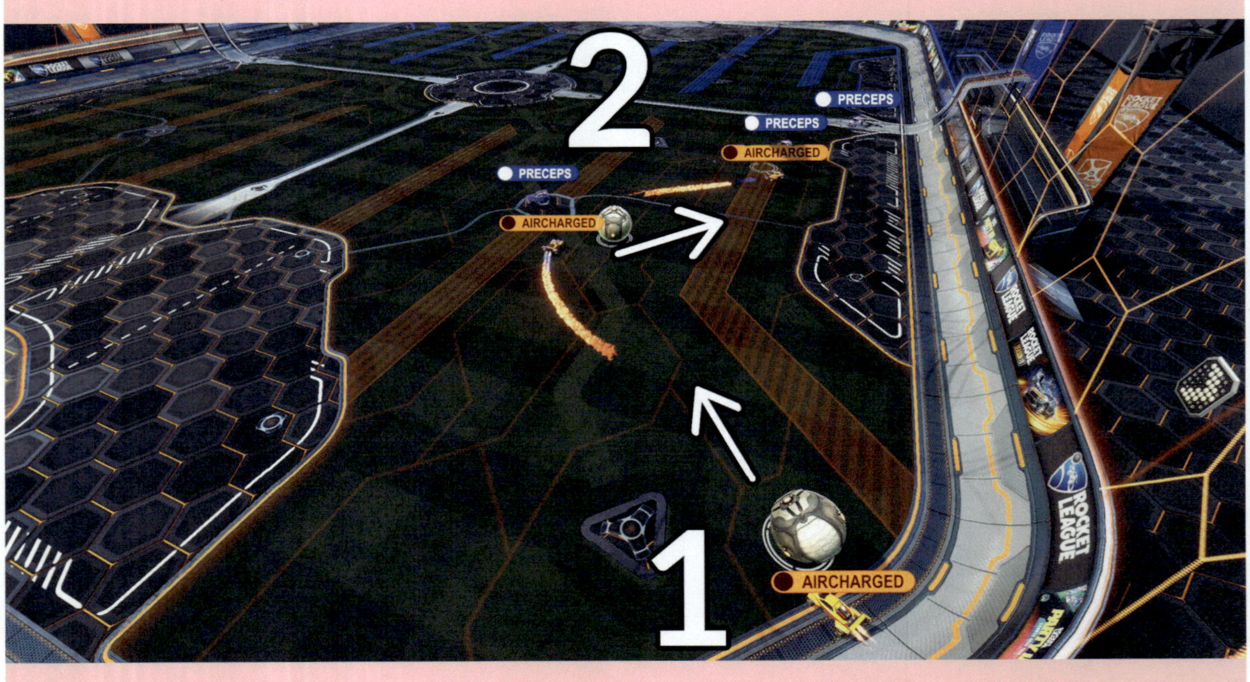

Drill 15A - Instant Flick

- **Setup:** Solo drill in Free Play. Start with the ball near your car. **Press down on the D-pad** to place it close, then press **right on the D-pad** to pop the ball into the air.
- As the ball rises and falls, stay in **car cam** to keep your forward view, and position your car **just inside the white circle** on the ground.
- When the ball is falling into range, **jump high**, then perform a **front flip** to strike the ball with the **tail of your car**.
- Experiment with different timings and positions within the circle to vary the **height** and **power** of the flick.

Drill 16A - Jab

- **Setup:** Solo drill in Free Play. Reset the ball and begin **pushing it slowly away** from the goal you want to attack.
- **Speed ahead of the ball**, then use a **power slide turn** to quickly face back toward it.
- As the ball rolls toward you, **drive into it with boost**, striking it cleanly to **jab the ball high**, ideally aiming to score.
- The focus is on **creating vertical lift**, not power. The goal is to train the instinct to lift the ball into the air and begin your attack with purpose.

Drill 17A - Bounce Dribble

- **Setup:** Solo drill in Free Play. Start in the corner, as if setting up a lateral dribble.
- Lateral dribble the ball and after it goes past the centre, begin fading to the outside.
- Start dribbling by **guiding the ball from the outside**, letting it **bounce naturally** as you move toward the goal.
- Use **light, side-on touches** with the part of your car you would use in a power slide cut to **redirect the ball gently** after each bounce.
- Avoid holding boost, stay grounded and focus on using **angle and timing** to slowly bring the ball inward toward a shot position.
- The goal is to maintain **complete control** while allowing the ball to bounce between each touch. This sets up power shots, fakes, flicks, and 50/50s without losing rhythm or boost.

Drill 17B - Power Shot (Rising)

- **Setup:** Solo drill in Free Play. Start in the corner, as if setting up a lateral dribble.
- Lateral dribble the ball and after it goes past the centre, begin fading to the outside.
- Let the ball **bounce naturally**, using soft side touches with the car to guide it around from the outside.
- As the ball **rises off the bounce**, strike it with the **inside front corner** of your car using a controlled **side flip.**
- The goal is to **launch the ball toward the far post** with a clean hit off the bounce, without overusing boost.

Drill 17C - Power Shot (Falling)

- **Setup:** Solo drill in Free Play. Start in the corner, as if setting up a lateral dribble.
- Lateral dribble the ball and after it goes past the centre, begin fading to the outside.
- Let the ball **bounce naturally**, using soft side touches with the car to guide it around from the outside.
- Let the ball **rise and begin to fall**, then aim to side flip so that as the car rotates in the side flip the ball is hit with the **outside front corner** of your car.
- Aim to **slot the ball into the near post** or across goal, depending on your angle and timing.
- The goal is to disguise your timing and use the **fall of the bounce** to generate power and break rhythm.

Drill 18A - Trailer

- **Setup:** Two-player drill. Player A starts with the ball at mid boost. Player B behind and central, applying string theory.
- Player A begins dribbling the ball diagonally toward the middle, **leading the ball slightly away from themselves** and **closer to Player B**.
- As Player A moves the ball into a hittable position for Player B, they **peel off** and drive toward the backline, looking to **bump or demo the nearest defender**.
- Player B reads the setup and **instantly reacts**, either going for a jab if the net is defended or taking a **safe 50/50** if pressure is incoming.
- Run the drill repeatedly, alternating trailer and first man roles. Focus on **reading the play, adjusting timing**, and being **decisive under pressure**.

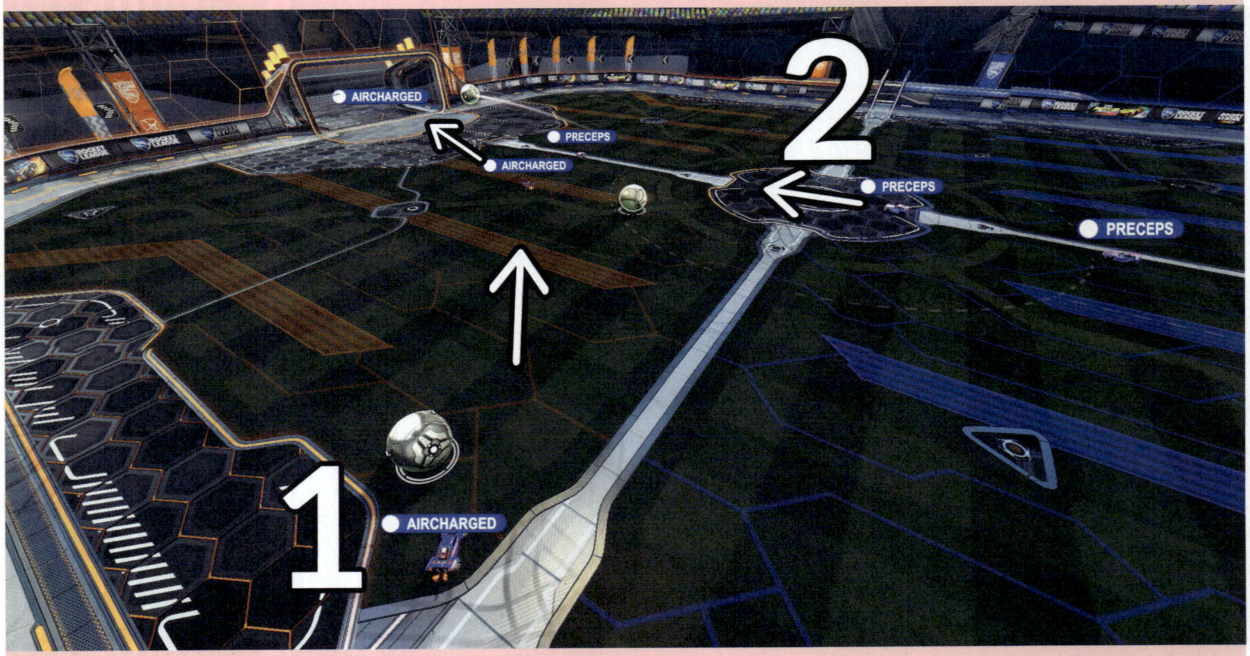

Drill 19A - Pacifist Pivot Wrap

- **Setup:** Two-player drill. Player A starts with the ball in the opponent's corner. Player B waits near **pad 1 or pad 2**, ready to receive a back pass.
- Player A begins by **wrapping around the ball**, then **dragging or tapping it backward** into the middle of the field toward Player B.
- The pass should be **grounded or bouncing gently**, giving Player B a perfect chance to jab the ball upward into the next phase.
- Player B **jabs the ball upward instantly** on arrival, beginning the next attacking phase.
- After jabbing, Player B **drives at the net**, then **peels off to grab a free corner boost pad** (whichever side has not been taken).
- While that's happening, Player A, now near pad 1 or 2, **re-jabs the ball** after it bounces off the **backboard.**
- Repeat the cycle, alternating jab, rotate, boost, and backboard follow-up.

Drill 19B - Pacifist Pivot Push

- **Setup:** Two-player drill. Player A starts with the ball in the **opponent's corner**, on one side of the field. Player B waits near **pad 1 or pad 2** in the centre.
- Player A **hits the ball over the face of the opponent's net**, into the **opposite corner**. Use the natural momentum to **wrap around the ball** and play a clean **drag-back or soft back pass** into midfield.
- Player B waits patiently, then **jabs the ball upward** as it arrives, becoming the new 1st man.
- After the jab, Player B **drives forward toward net**, then **peels off** and collects the **nearest free corner boost pad**.
- Meanwhile, Player A, now rotating out to pad 1 or 2, will **re-jab the ball** after it **bounces off the backboard**, continuing the rhythm.
- Repeat the full cycle. Focus on **natural momentum, clean pivots**, and **maintaining flow** between both players.

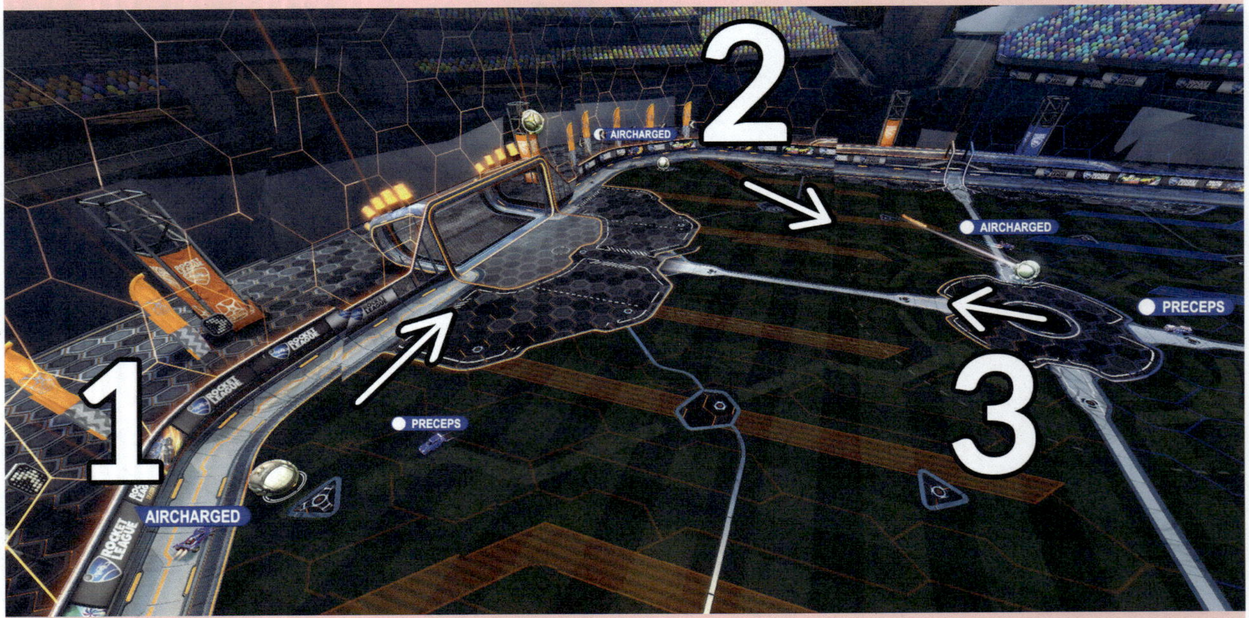

YOU MADE IT

You have reached the end of The Ultimate Rocket League 2v2 Guide, **The Pacifist System**.

This was not just a guide, it was a system.
A complete shift in how you approach the game. With control, intention, and clarity.

If you have followed the blueprints, run the drills, and truly embraced the mindset, then you have already done what most players never do.

You have slowed the game down, and started playing it on your terms.

But this is only the beginning.

I am currently pushing toward Supersonic Legend, applying everything in this book at the highest level. And as that journey continues, I will be building an advanced Pacifist System, for those who want to master the game beyond Grand Champion.

If that sounds like something you would be interested in, or if you want to keep learning, training, or even get coached directly:

Join the community at:

www.airchargedrl.com

(Or scan the QR code below to hop into Discord.)

You are now part of a system that has taken players all the way to Grand Champ, and you are not done yet.

See you on the field.

– AirCharged

WITH THANKS

With thanks to everyone who has purchased this book to help support myself, my channel and The Pacifist System.

It has been a long road, full of testing, reviewing, updating, and more testing. This project has been in the works for years, and it is still evolving. I am beyond grateful to everyone who helped bring it to life.

Special thanks to those who directly contributed to this book:

- **Buffalumps**
- **Hollowpoint**
- **F_U_Z_E**
- **Ultimo**
- **Preceps**

Thanks to every single person who has every purchased coaching, and especially people who have taken part in The Pacifist System to help advance it and spread it even more.

With heartfelt thanks to:

- **JustSpirit** - Without him there would be no community. He was my first ever viewer on Twitch and pushed me to make a Discord and create YouTube videos, he had the vision.
- **Raidmeister** - The greatest player & brain I got to play with and bounce ideas off. Also extremely open minded and helped me see how the ideas would work amongst the top 50 players in the world.
- **McLobe** - Part of the original testing team, a true gent, and part of RLBC.
- **Chaingun** - Part of the original crew of testing. Best marbles streams, great guy.
- **Max** - One of the OG's that helped a lot with hype moments on twitch and promotion.
- **Dreamy** - My first coaching client, taught me a lot about building a community.
- **Sandreeche** - My longest coaching client, helped me more than he will ever know.
- **Kal** - Gave me the confidence in my coaching and running the business side.
- **Preceps** - The assistant coach on The Pacifist System live cohorts, training partner, teammate and all around incredible guy.
- **Buffalumps -** A great guy and supporter, has given me so much advice and book recommendations.

There are many, many more people I could thank, but I am running out of space. Just know I appreciate every single one of you. Thank you all.

SPECIAL OFFER

Thank you for supporting The Pacifist System!

As a book owner, you have unlocked two exclusive rewards:

Coaching Discount

Get 20% off your next coaching session or package.

How to claim:

1. Join the official Pacifist System Discord.
2. Send a photo of your copy of this book to the #book-owners channel
3. You will be added to a spreadsheet gaining you 20% off your next coaching purchase, any type, any tier.

Secret Merch Drop

Access the hidden ZaZaZa. merch page, only for book owners.
From belt badges to exclusive designs, this collection is not listed anywhere else.

Visit: airchargedrl.com#bookbonus
(or scan the QR code below)

Made in the USA
Monee, IL
09 June 2026

52810856R00081